T0323468

Global Business in the Age of Transformation

Global Business in the Age of Transformation

Mahesh K. Joshi and J.R. Klein

OXFORD
UNIVERSITY PRESS

OXFORD
UNIVERSITY PRESS

Great Clarendon Street, Oxford, OX2 6DP,
United Kingdom

Oxford University Press is a department of the University of Oxford.
It furthers the University's objective of excellence in research, scholarship,
and education by publishing worldwide. Oxford is a registered trade mark of
Oxford University Press in the UK and in certain other countries

First Edition published in 2021

Published in the United States of America by Oxford University Press
198 Madison Avenue, New York, NY 10016, United States of America

British Library Cataloguing in Publication Data
Data available

Library of Congress Control Number: 2021910169

ISBN 978-0-19-284723-2

DOI: 10.1093/oso/9780192847232.001.0001

Printed and bound in the UK by
TJ Books Limited

Foreword

This book is a timely one. We have witnessed , as we have struggled to cope with a pandemic, how interconnected and interdependent we are as human beings. The book considers how our increasing interconnection impacts the world's economies, regulation, geopolitical issues, and market sectors. The role of technology in facilitating and compromising interconnectedness is explored and the book is noteworthy for the careful discussion of barriers to interconnection. The authors are to be congratulated in the way in which they have conducted their research that underpins each chapter. They have not simply relied on written evidence but have sought to have conversations with academics, practitioners, and practical thinkers to ensure that existing written evidence is explored critically with people on the ground.

There are several chapters that focus on what a more interconnected world means for leadership practices going forward. The authors highlight the importance of introspection and curiosity in leadership work. This curiosity is not limited to market or sector contexts but involves finding time to pause and consider your own journey as a leader, what your followers want from the world of work, and crucially to explore the complexity of the contexts of which you are a part. Leaders are accountable but they are not in control, so understanding what needs to be done to build an agile organization and unleash leadership energy throughout the organization is critical. This requires a shift for leaders to think more deeply about the ecosystem they inhabit and the chapters in this book enable such reflection.

Global Business in the Age of Transformation is a straightforward, readable commentary on the intricacies and impacts of globalization in transition. It examines trends, provides insight, and suggests approaches for survival in the dramatically changing business world. The authors present a balanced and simple explanation of the changing face of global business, how it is affecting everyone, and makes recommendations for change strategies. It highlights how geo-political upheavals impact business, hyper dynamic technology, leadership, and emerging economies. The book should encourage thinking and conversations about where we are and inspire realistic reflection and opportunities for business success in a global world.

The book's topics are relevant to readers in developed, developing, and undeveloped areas around the world. It has special appeal in emerging economies that are in the midst of technology-driven changes creating an egalitarian ethos that have the potential for changing everything everywhere. It is pertinent to pre-academic and academic learners, business leaders, and the general public interested in the topic of globalism and seeking understanding of its effects and how to deal with them. It provides not only an unpretentious explanation of major world changes and how they play out in local communities, but also useful ideas on staying relevant.

This is a book that will change the way you think.

Professor Sue Dopson
Interim Dean
Said Business School
University of Oxford

Preface

I sat there staring at it for a long time. It had been hanging there for a while and I'd walked by it numerous times, some with little notice and some with extended study. A gift from a good friend from Australia, it was a mandala. This particular style of painting is meant to represent a picture of feeling, emotion, self-reconstruction, the universe that though not abstract in design provides a circular presentation of geometric shapes that for some reason, today, just did not look right. There was something about it that I had felt before that was now much more insistent. What was it? The 'raison d'être', the purpose, just did not feel right. It was somehow incomplete, like there was more it was trying to offer but I just could not see it. As I reached into this mysterious cognizant problem, my wife passed behind me and with little more than a glance at my state of dismay, moved out of the room almost out of range and with her back to me made an offhand almost cavalier comment, 'You know that's upside down, don't you?'

My mandala experience has a cognitive connection to the way many process the hyperdynamic speed of change in a world that is not yet finished its process of getting smaller. There seems to be an almost unidentified perplexity that is an opportunity for some and a consternation for others.

Karl Schoemer in his book *The New Reality: How to Make Change Your Competitive Advantage*, states: 'Change is impartial. It cares not a whit about corporate reputation, size, previous successes, or prestige. It rewards only those who meet it head on. All change is about movement – individual movement, organizational movement. As individuals we must move away from danger and toward opportunity, and we must do so consistently and quickly. The organization, in turn, must be filled with people doing the same – moving quickly and consistently toward opportunity, toward the customer, toward the marketplace.' It is critical that businesses big and small with leaders old and new continually move forward. The jaws of change will bite us if we run from it but if we stand still, they will eat us alive.

The key to dealing with this globalized mandala in its complex abstract design is to focus on staying relevant. In the *Global Business in the Age of Transformation* we examine the world in the throes of metamorphic transformation by heat and pressure that is reshaping local and global economies, geopolitical landscapes, technological impact, and challenging the very definition of leadership.

J.R. Klein
Principal, J.R. Global

Contents

SECTION 1
STRUCTURAL TRANSFORMATION

1

The Global Phenomenon

The phenomenon of globalization has been acknowledged and debated for decades and some might argue for centuries. What seems to be a result of the natural curiosity of the human species has resulted in their movement and interaction with geographies, cultures, and communities different than their own. Globalization's interpretation and conversations vary from firm confidence that the world's interconnectivity has prehistoric roots to the conviction that the phenomenon is a relatively recent experience.

Examining this global interconnective state, and most specifically its effect on business, was the topic of our previous book, *Global Business*. It looked at the impact of a world seeking to grasp the ramifications of the explosion of technology and information. It explored the influence of this transformation on economies, business sectors, governments, countries, and cultures. This book follows that discussion with detailed thinking about the transformation itself.

As some voices debate the demise of globalization and postulate about a return to former borders and glories, the realities of the world present the undeniable truth that we are all in this together. Unfortunately, it takes a crisis to move us from where we are. The COVID-19 pandemic in 2020 has served that function. What started in December of 2019 as an isolated cluster of cases of pneumonia in Wuhan, China, moved to a worldwide epidemic crisis in April of 2020 with over 3 million cases and 215,000 deaths (World Health Organization, 2020). Almost every country in the world was impacted and the realities of the global transformation became shockingly evident.

Global Business in the Age of Transformation. Mahesh K. Joshi and J.R. Klein, Oxford University Press.
© Mahesh K. Joshi and J.R. Klein 2021. DOI: 10.1093/oso/9780192847232.003.0001

As we restart our thinking on globalization it is beneficial to explore its origins as a basis for the study of today's transformational environment. The initial consideration is the subtlety of terminology.

Is there a difference between globalism and globalization? At its essence globalism attempts to describe how basic human curiosity blossomed into a world characterized by interconnectivity involving networks of connections that reach every corner of the globe. The globalism narrative seeks to understand the interconnections of today's world and identify patterns that explain them. Globalism is not universal.

In this definitional arena, globalization describes the dynamic growth or retraction in the level of globalism. In short, consider globalism as the underlying basic network, while globalization refers to the dynamic shrinking of distance on a large scale (Nye, 2002). This narrative concentrates on the factors impacting the changes and the speed of those changes.

Globalism

Globalism traces its origin to basic human curiosity and therefore is as old as humanity itself. Since the first human decided to see what was over the hill, mankind has attempted to satisfy its curiosity and expand its power, spread its faith, and improve its quality of life by exploring the environment. The resulting interaction, whether peaceful or forceful, produced a basic sharing of ideas, commodities, capital, and people.

In the search for food, shelter, and land humans moved outside their basic point of origin to every corner of the globe. This journey has led to revelation upon revelation and change upon change. From the taming of fire to the idea of the wheel, the evolution of society from hunter-gatherers to a settled agricultural way of life, and the creation of the written word, humans have explored the unexplored world. Their methodology was trial and error and as it progressed the value of discoveries and innovations continued to move the 'intuitive mucking about' into new geographies and populations whether established or conquered.

As patterns diversified and developed they grew into early civilizations, such as in Mesopotamia and the Indus Valley. These civilizations fostered the rise of cities and city-states, the evolution of the diversification of work and job specialists, and social classes.

As globalism progressed it resulted in three basic changes. First, the rise of the West and the fall of the East. Secondly, technology is the driver of change. Thirdly, the cultural impact of the spread of religion. Over a few hundred years, Islam, empowered by military technology, expanded from its place of origin in the Arabian peninsula all the way to modern Spain in the West, and northern India in the East (Kant, 2019).

It is important to note that globalism does not imply universality. The connections that make up the networks that define globalism may be felt more strongly in some parts of the world than in others. For example, at the turn of the twenty-first century, a quarter of the US population used the World Wide Web. At the same time, however, only one-hundredth of one per cent of the population of South Asia had access to this information network (Nye, 2002). In this definition, globalism is not universal.

Globalization

There is an ongoing debate over the historical origins of globalization. Some scholars place its origins in the modern era, others regard it as a result of a long history. Some authors have argued that stretching the beginning of globalization far back in time renders the concept wholly inoperative and useless for political analysis (Conversi, 2010).

For those scholars who say that the roots of modern globalization can be found as early as the prehistoric period, territorial expansion to all five continents is a key factor in the formation of globalization. The development of agriculture furthered globalization by converting the vast majority of the world's population into a settled lifestyle. Globalization failed to accelerate due to the lack of long-distance interaction and technology (Steger, 2009).

Other scholars start globalization in the early modern period of history, which follows the late Middle Ages. There are varied chronological limits of the period that are open to debate, including the Ottoman conquest of Constantinople in 1453, the Renaissance period in Europe and Timurid Central Asia, the Muslim conquests in the Indian subcontinent, the Age of Discovery (Christopher Columbus 1492, Vasco da Gama 1498) and the Age of Revolutions (c.1800) (O'Rourke and Williamson, 2002). Reader interest and further study of these progressive globalization steps are encouraged.

Common ground in this debate can be found around the middle of the nineteenth century as increased capital and labour mobility coupled with decreased transport costs led to a smaller world. It was the Industrial Revolution during the nineteenth century that spurred the formation of globalization as the dynamic force we recognize today. Industrialization allowed standardized production of household items using economies of scale while rapid population growth created sustained demand for commodities. Steamships reduced the cost of international transport significantly and railroads made inland transportation cheaper. The transport revolution occurred sometime between 1820 and 1850. More nations embraced international trade. Globalization in this period was decisively shaped by nineteenth-century imperialism such as in Africa and Asia (O'Rourke and Williamson, 2002).

After the Second World War, work by politicians led to the agreements of the Bretton Woods Conference, in which major governments laid down the framework for international monetary policy, commerce, and finance, and the founding of several international institutions intended to facilitate economic growth by lowering trade barriers. Initially, the General Agreement on Tariffs and Trade (GATT) led to a series of agreements to remove trade restrictions. GATT's successor was the World Trade Organization (WTO), which provided a framework for negotiating and formalizing trade agreements and a dispute resolution process. Exports nearly doubled from 8.5 per cent of total gross world product in 1970 to 16.2 per cent in 2001. The approach of using global agreements to advance trade stumbled with the failure of the Doha Development Round (2001) of trade negotiation. Many countries then shifted to bilateral or smaller multilateral agreements, such as the 2011 South Korea–United States Free Trade Agreement (Global Policy Forum, 2008).

The DH Comet, the world's first commercial jet airliner, entered service in 1949 and by the 1970s flying had become affordable to the growing middle classes in developed countries. A global open skies policy and the availability of low-cost carriers brought competition to the market. The growth of low-cost communication networks, in the 1990s, reduced the expense of communicating between countries. The third phase of the Industrial Revolution enabled work to be done using a computer regardless of location. After the Second World War, student exchange programmes intended to increase understanding and tolerance of other cultures, improve language skills, and broaden social horizons became the vanguard of global travel (Varghese, 2008).

Since the 1980s, modern globalization has spread rapidly through the expansion of capitalism and neoliberal ideologies (Benería, 2016). The enactment of policies enabled the deregulation of laws that opened markets, privatized public industry, and caused a reduction in governmental social services. These policies were offered to developing countries and were implemented by the World Bank and the International Monetary Fund (IMF). The programmes required that the country receiving monetary aid would open its markets to capitalism, privatize public industry, allow free trade, cut social services like healthcare and education, and allow the free movement of giant multinational corporations (Benería, 2016). The implementation of these programmes established the World Bank and the IMF as global financial market regulators and the creation of free markets for multinational corporations on a global scale.

The interconnectivity of the world's economies and cultures grew very quickly in the late nineteenth and early twentieth centuries but slowed through the world war and Cold War years (1910s–70s). By 1980 the trend was reversing toward the upheavals of 1989, signalling considerable expansion of global interconnectedness. The migration and movement of people can also be highlighted as a prominent feature of the globalization process. In the period between 1965 and 1990, the proportion of the labour force migrating approximately doubled. Most migration occurred between the developing countries and least developed countries (Saggi, 2002).

Economic access encouraged the movement of workers from low wage countries to higher wage areas and their movement to the international market economy offered by the developing world. It also allowed for the increasing movement of diseases across borders and continents, the spread of culture and consumer values, the growing importance of international institutions like the United Nations (UN), and international cooperation on shared issues like the environment and human rights.

Other changes as dramatic included the Internet becoming important in connecting people from around the world. As of April 2020, more than 4.57 billion (59 per cent) have access to the Internet (Statista, 2020). Global accessibility has become seamless. Today's interconnected societies have myriad opportunities and options for cultures, groups, ideologies, and markets to shrink the distance that separate them.

Both globalism and globalization are all too often defined in strictly economic terms as if the world economy as such defined globalism. But other forms are equally important. There are four distinct dimensions of globalism: economic, military, environmental—and social (Nye, 2002). For our purpose as a delineation of the legacy of globalization, we will deal with economics, culture, and politics.

Economic—Trade

We hesitate to classify economics as a driver of the global phenomenon, but it is at the very least a primary driver of benefits and negative consequences of the dynamic change. As we have discovered, globalization has opened borders and streamlined communications including business transactions. It has increased reciprocally advantageous relations between countries enabling goods and services and capital to flow freely. In the changing character of the market, it could be viewed as congenial partnerships that strengthen the global economy in a world destined for harmony. The benefits of increased globalization are many, but for businesses especially small businesses, there is also a negative side.

Local Business

The issue of market dumping or oversupply: The outstanding issues and anxieties of the global presence of big business are the obstacles smaller businesses face when competing with large-scale businesses that offer consumer goods. For example, almost every country has to compete with China's ability to produce and mass export goods at prices that are virtually impossible to match, which can make maintaining the viability of local businesses challenging. Regardless of the local availability of custom problem solving and quick and available customer service, it is difficult to compete with low-priced products.

Some service industries also feel the effect. Online and phone-based consumer support businesses can find it hard to compete with foreign markets. It is the concept of implementation of better service that can keep local business relevant. It may not be viable to hire an electrician from another country, but many consumers will contend with below-standard remote services if it means saving some money. Local strategies must focus on the customer experience as a way to remain alive.

Global market chain changes: The challenge of dealing with the way that business works in this new environment can be overwhelming. The irritation of large-scale changes on local customer attitudes, fluctuations in costs of raw materials, and even the slightest change from local suppliers can drive business to far-off competitors.

Though it seems infeasible, because of the interconnected nature of the market local businesses have to deal with some of the larger economic concerns. Just as large corporations are impacted by multi-country concerns, the uncertainty of faraway decisions, such as Brexit or trade wars, small businesses must be prepared to deal with the same surprises and unknowns and navigate the same foggy trail. Whether it is trade wars, market fluctuations, border closing, or pandemics, businesses must be flexible to remain feasible.

The competition has changed: There was a time when maintaining a robust presence in a community was easier for a local business because of the state of access to technology and information along with the parochial character of business within defined boundaries. In today's world, any consumer good can be simply and quickly ordered online and delivered directly to the doorstep. Local presence may still be a viable though outdated physical construct but it has little validity in a virtual marketplace. Global entities are designing commodities and services to particular segments of local markets that make it tough for a small business to compete. It is no longer simply an issue of cost, but rather of how a large corporation with access to proper research, data, and manufacturing facilities can blot out a local market (Piletic, 2018).

Work and the Workplace

The world of work has been impacted by technology. Work is different than it was in the past due to digital innovation. Labour market opportunities are becoming polarized between high-end and low-end skilled jobs. Migration and its effects on employment have become a sensitive political issue. From Buffalo to Beijing, public debates are raging about the future of work. Development in automation like artificial intelligence and machine intelligence is contributing to productivity, efficiency, safety, and convenience but is also having an impact on jobs, skills, wages, and the nature of work. The 'undiscovered country' of the workplace today is the combination of the changing landscape of work itself and the availability of ill-fitting tools, platforms, and knowledge to train for the requirements, skills, and structure of this new age (Joshi and Klein, 2018).

Entrepreneurship has enabled newcomers to successfully challenge existing large corporations during the transition from the industrial to the digital era. Entrepreneurs take their creations online instantly instead of the conventional method of starting in a local geography and expanding into international markets.

Digital economy, globalization, and entrepreneurship have become interwoven factors. With the support of capital from venture capital funds, they are not only driving creative destruction of the existing and developing new things but also developing new business models, ideas to make new products and develop new technologies. Silicon Valley provides an example of an ecosystem required for successfully breeding entrepreneurship with its education system, cutting-edge research, culture, acceptance of failure, and availability of finance. Entrepreneurial development in the digital age has moved from the development of hardware and software platforms to the creation of and access to technology platforms and the development of new business models. Replication of new business models is now almost instantaneous (Joshi and Klein, 2018).

New technologies like artificial intelligence, robotics, machine intelligence, and the Internet of Things are seeing repetitive tasks move away from humans to machines. Humans cannot become machines, but machines can become more human-like.

Today's addition to this continuum is that technology has enhanced the pace of innovation and the need for focused learning in new skill areas. It has become necessary to avoid becoming irrelevant tomorrow. The normal life cycle of workers has been to consume a lifetime's worth of preparation in the first few years of life and for the rest of the time draw down on that depositary. This traditional model is fast becoming irrelevant. Now the model is to learn, work, and enjoy at the same time. This is creating a massive need for retooling of existing human workers.

Another major issue for humans is the need to train their minds to remain focused in a society which is constantly bombarded with information at a frantic pace. It seems like we may have to become a sort of corporate yogi with the spiritual and mental capacity to start with, unlike a corporate athlete. Corporate athletes began with building physical capacity, then emotional and mental capacity and finally the spiritual capacity. The two starting factors of physical and mental capacity are slowly being taken away by machines and artificial intelligence. The order of capacity building is almost reversed now with a starting point of building your spiritual capacity like a yogi to avoid distractions created by technology in order to build mental and physical capacity (Joshi and Klein, 2018).

Trade

Shoppers are demanding the instantaneous connectivity and one-click convenience to which they have become accustomed. Access to online commerce through the provisions of a technological revolution is at the heart of cross-border trade. At the junction sits the consumer. Most consumers have already experienced the online shopping experience with immediate, frictionless, payments, and they are not prepared to settle for anything less. In short, they are not prepared to tolerate a service that does not deliver this type of experience. If services do not match expectations, the consumers will simply move their consumption elsewhere. In an increasingly globalized world, this does not mean just within their country, but internationally (Ideas Magazine, 2019).

Cultural

Culture is the character of civilization. It involves the expected social behaviour, the standards, and customs as well as the knowledge, beliefs, laws, capabilities, arts, and habits of a unique group of people. Humans acquire culture through the learning processes of enculturation and socialization, which is shown by the diversity of cultures across societies.

In this arena as in many others in today's world of interconnectedness, the notion of autonomous, clearly defined, and stable cultures is unusual. The opportunities and open access available through elements of globalization are drawing people from diverse cultural backgrounds into strong relationships. This is also evidenced in the extraordinary expansion of tourism and the prosperity of multinational corporations, and the development of new cross-border agreements like the European Community, the Association of Southeast Asian Nations (ASEAN), and the Canada–United States–Mexico Agreement. The diffusion of various elements of culture is evidenced by the spread of pop culture, migrations, the proliferation of online communities, and the creation of global institutions like the IMF, World Trade Organization (WTO), and the World Bank. Despite the perception that cultural globalization fosters instability in change, the most significant effects are being observed in global thinking of local communities.

The phrase 'cultural globalization' describes migration and osmoses of ideas and values on a global scale supporting the growth and strength of social relationships. It is evidenced in the common acceptance of cultures and the processes of commodity exchange and colonization that have a long history of disseminating cultural influence around the globe.

The circulation of cultures enables individuals to partake in extended social relations that cross national and regional borders. The creation and expansion of such social relations are not merely observed on a material level. Cultural globalization involves the formation of shared norms and knowledge with which people associate their individual and collective cultural identities. It brings increasing interconnectedness among different populations and cultures. (Steger, 2009).

Political

Political globalization describes the growth of the worldwide political system that is accompanied by the declining importance of the nation-state and the emergence of new actors on the political scene. Like globalization itself, political globalization has several dimensions and lends itself to several interpretations. It has been discussed in the context of new emancipatory possibilities, as well as in the context of loss of autonomy and fragmentation of the social world (Delanty and Rumford, 2008).

Political globalization can be seen in changes such as the democratization of the world, creation of the global civil society, and moving beyond the centrality of the nation-state, particularly as the sole actor in the field of politics. Some of the questions central to the discussion of political globalization are related to the future of the nation-state, whether its importance is diminishing, what are the causes for those changes, and understanding the emergence of the concept of global governance (Steger, 2003) The creation and existence of the UN have been called one of the classic examples of political globalization. Political actions by non-governmental organizations and social movements, concerned about various topics such as environmental protection, are another example (Mooney and Evans, 2007).

Here we have taken a quick survey of the history of globalization. The next task is to look at the process of transformation itself. The beginning of that journey opens by examining the evidence and transactions of the transformation within the continually advancing phenomenon of globalization.

Bibliography

Benería, L. (2016). *Gender, Development, and Globalization: Economics as if All People Mattered*. New York: Routledge.

Conversi, D. (2010). The limits of cultural globalisation. *Journal of Critical Globalisation Studies*, 3, 36–59.

Delanty, G. and Rumford, C. (2008). Political globalization. In G. Ritzer (ed.), *The Blackwell Companion to Globalization* (pp. 414–28). Malden, MA: Blackwell.

Faiola, A. (2009). A global retreat as economies dry up. *The Washington Post*, 5 March.

Global Policy Forum (2008). *World Exports as Percentage of Gross World Product*. New York: Global Policy Forum.

Gregory, P. R. and Stuart, R. C. (2013). *The Global Economy and its Economic Systems*. Boston: South-Western Cengage Learning.

Ideas Magazine (2019). The rising challenges and opportunities of cross-border trade. *International Finance*, 18 April. https://internationalfinance.com/the-rising-challenges-and-opportunities-of-cross-border-trade/.

International Monetary Fund (2007). *World Economic Outlook 2007.* Washington, DC: International Monetary Fund.

James, P. and Steger, M. B. (eds.) (2010). *Globalization and Culture, Volume 4: Ideologies of Globalism.* London: Sage Publications.

Joshi, M. K. and Klein, J. R. (2018). *Global Business.* Oxford: Oxford University Press.

Kant, V. (2019). When did globalization begin? *Global Shapers Annual Summit.* Geneva: World Economic Forum. https://www.weforum.org/agenda/2019/01/when-did-globalization-begin-the-answer-might-surprise-you/.

Levinson, M. (2013). *The Box: How the Shipping Container Made the World Smaller and the World Economy Bigger.* Princeton, NJ: Princeton University Press.

McKinsey Global Institute (2014). *Global Flows in a Digital Age: How Trade, Finance, People, and Data Connect the World.* New York: McKinsey Global Institute.

McKinsey Global Institute (2016). *Digital Globalization: The New Era of Global Flows.* New York: McKinsey Global Institute.

McKinsey Global Institute (2017). *Foreign Affairs.* New York: McKinsey Global Institute.

Mooney, A. and Evans, B. (eds.) (2007). *Globalization: The Key Concepts.* Abingdon: Routledge.

Nye, J. (2002). What are the different spheres of globalism – and how are they affected by globalization? *The Globalist*, 15 April. https://www.the-globalist.com/globalism-versus-globalization/.

O'Rourke, K. and Williamson, J. G. (2002). When did globalization begin? *European Review of Economic History*, 6(1), 23–50.

Piletic, P. (2018). How globalization impacts small businesses more than you might think. *Customer Think*, 28 June. https://customerthink.com/how-globalization-impacts-small-businesses-more-than-you-might-think/.

Saggi, K. (2002). Trade, foreign direct investment, and international technology transfer: A survey. *World Bank Research Observer*, 1 September, 191–235.

Statista (2020). Global digital population as of April 2020. *Statista*, April. https://www.statista.com/statistics/617136/digital-population-worldwide/.

Steger, M. B. (2003). *Globalization: A Very Short Introduction.* Oxford: Oxford University Press.

Steger, M. B. (2009). *Globalization: A Very Short Introduction*, 2nd edition. Oxford: Oxford University Press.

The Economist (2014). Signs of life. *The Economist*, 13 November.

The Open Market Internet Index (1995). *Treese*, 11 November. https://web. archive.org/web/20130601045949/http://www.treese.org/intindex/ 95-11.htm.

Varghese, N. (2008). *Globalization of Higher Education and Cross-Border Student Mobility*. Paris: International Institute for Educational Planning, UNESCO.

Vries, J. D. (2010). The limits of globalization in the early modern world. *Economic History Review*, 63(3), 710–33.

Wintour, P. (2020). Coronavirus: Who will be winners and losers in the new world order? *The Guardian*, 11 April.

World Health Organization (2020). *Situation Report 98*. World Health Organization, 27 April. https://www.who.int/emergencies/diseases/ novel-coronavirus-2019/situation-reports/.

World Stats (2012). Internet World Stats, Miniwatts Marketing Group, 30 June. https://www.internetworldstats.com/stats.htm.

2
Economic Clusters and Emerging Players

Conversations in the global environment of real-time dialogue often centre on developed markets, developing markets, and emerging markets. Those discussions are full of acronyms that can lead to a good deal of confusion. This discussion begins with a 'cheat sheet' on what all this means. Much of the nomenclature is used to frame clusters of markets. The alphabet soup includes BRICS, TIMP, MINT, N11, and Frontier Markets each representing a group of emerging economies usually, but not always, defined by similarities in development status.

- BRICS: Brazil, Russia, India, China, and South Africa (O'Neill, 2001)
- TIMP: Turkey, Indonesia, Mexico, and the Philippines (Aenlle, 2013)
- MINT: Mexico, Indonesia, Nigeria, and Turkey (Kenton, 2019)
- N11: Bangladesh, Egypt, Indonesia, Iran, Mexico, Nigeria, Pakistan, the Philippines, Turkey, South Korea, and Vietnam (Donev et al., 2020)
- Frontier Markets: A frontier market is a type of developing country which is more developed than the least developed countries, but too small to be generally considered an emerging market. (Musacchio and Werker, 2016)

These future growth market acronyms subtly tell another story and that is evidenced by the fact that the centre of gravity of the world's economy is shifting towards the East. The acronyms and the

Global Business in the Age of Transformation. Mahesh K. Joshi and J.R. Klein, Oxford University Press.
© Mahesh K. Joshi and J.R. Klein 2021. DOI: 10.1093/oso/9780192847232.003.0002

emerging economies represented may be real growth opportunities for businesses or just reflect the excitement created by financial institutions to sell investment funds and enticing people to invest. Regardless of the outcome, the background of these economic clusters is important to examine.

BRICS

BRICS countries represent almost 40 per cent of the world's population with over 3 billion people (Plecher, 2020b) along with their increasing spending power and role in international affairs. They are all part of the G20[1] with recognized potential for huge growth and are the focus of much speculation. '[T]he five BRICS countries together account for almost a quarter of the Earth's landmass, more than 40 percent of the world's population, and 46 percent of the world's labor force. BRICS countries are credited for nearly 30 percent of global gross domestic product and almost 50 percent of the global economic growth' (Al-Mohamad et al., 2020).

The term BRIC was coined by Jim O'Neill, an economist at Goldman Sachs in a report in 2001 (O'Neill, 2001). O'Neill was inspired to create the acronym after the terrorist attacks of 11 September, 2001. He told the *Financial Times* (Tett, 2010) 'What 9/11 told me was that there was no way that globalisation was going to be Americanisation in the future, nor should it be... in order for globalisation to advance, it had to be accepted by more people... but not by imposing the dominant American social and philosophical beliefs and structures'. At that time Brazil, Russia, India, and China represented 8 per cent of the global economy. The theory was that these countries should be treated as a linked economic force driving the rise of emerging economies. BRIC became BRICS in 2010

---

[1] The Group of Twenty is an international forum for the governments and central bank governors from Argentina, Australia, Brazil, Canada, China, France, Germany, India, Indonesia, Italy, Japan, Mexico, Russian Federation, Saudi Arabia, South Africa, South Korea, Turkey, United Kingdom, United States, and the European Union. Founded in 1999, the G20 aims to discuss policy pertaining to the promotion of international financial stability (IPS News, 2015).

with the addition of South Africa. The popularity of BRICS over the next ten years attracted billions of dollars of investment by fund managers, consumer companies, and businesses. It led to the creation of its own investment fund.

In the decade after 2001, BRICS nations were enjoying the limelight and even started a BRICS bank, which only served to highlight their inability to do business together. According to the economic think tank Global Trade Alliance (Timmons, 2015), about a third of the time that commercial interests of BRICS nations were harmed, it was done by another BRICS nation. China's economy remains the most dominant of the BRICS nations. In 2018 it made up 16.34 per cent of the world's GDP, more than the combined GDPs of Brazil at 2.2 per cent, India at 7.74 per cent, Russia at 3.21 per cent, and South Africa at 0.43 per cent (The World Bank, 2019a).

BRICS Do Not Make a Wall

Thanks primarily to China, BRICS economies have done even better than forecasted; however, they are not without issues. Emerging markets have been through a great deal in recent years. The 'taper tantrum' in 2013 prompted by fears of a change in American monetary policy, the oil price drop in 2014, China's botched devaluation of its currency in 2015, and India's 'demonetization' of its currency in late 2016, when it removed high-value banknotes from circulation, have taken their toll.

In 2017, for the first time in several years, some growth in all BRICS countries was seen with the world's four biggest emerging economies all expanding at the same time. Russia's GDP bottomed out at the end of 2015 after the longest recession since the 1990s. During the collapse of the rouble in late 2014 and early 2015, it was easy to forget some of Russia's economic strengths. It has had a consistent trade surplus and a substantial foreign-exchange reserve, which never fell below $300 billion. As Russia has maintained its footing, the rouble has rebounded in value against the US dollar making it one of the world's best-performing currencies. Higher oil prices have also helped, although Russia cannot profit fully from the improved oil market by ramping up sales without violating the production limits that caused the market's recovery (Exchange Rates, 2020).

Brazil's torment has been even more prolonged. Its economy contracted for eight consecutive quarters as commodity prices tumbled, a president was impeached, and a corrupt political class was impugned. Brazil's political scandals are far from resolved, but the political climate has improved. Generous summer rains in states like Bahia contributed to a bumper harvest of soya beans and corn in the early months of 2017. However, bumper harvests cannot be repeated every three months; Brazil's GDP has fallen every year since, and many forecasters continue to voice only guarded optimism for positive growth.

Fast growth has not jeopardized Brazil's price stability but rather inflation has eased just as in Russia and India. Lower inflation and the Brazilian central bank's ability to make big interest rate cuts caused a political furore engulfing President Michel Temer who lost the 2018 election to Jair Bolsonaro who was sworn into office in January 2019. If President Bolsonaro's ultra conservative approach is successful in reforming social security and curbing fiscal excess, the central bank may soften its stance dramatically. The loosening of fiscal indiscipline, monetary easing, and a weakened currency will push prices up.

If inflation has been too high in recent years in Brazil it has been too low in China. Thanks to downward pressure on prices and the currency, China's economy shrank in dollar terms in 2016 for the first time in twenty-two years. But the deflationary threat has since receded and the yuan has strengthened against the greenback as capital outflows have been tamed. China's central bank may have resumed adding to its foreign-exchange reserves, which increased by $24 billion in May 2017, having declined by about $1 trillion since its 2014 peak as capital left the country (The World Bank, 2019a).

The resumption of growth in Brazil and Russia and the return of 'dollar growth' in China breathed new life into the BRICS brand. BRIC leaders began holding an annual summit and invited South Africa to join as an additional member. Initially, O'Neill felt that South Africa, a country of only 59.62 million people with a GDP of less than $360 billion (Focus Economics, 2020), was too small to stand alongside the original quartet. The fifth member's recent fortunes have diverged from the other BRICS nations as South Africa's economy slipped into a recession in the first quarter of 2017 (Focus Economics, 2020). BRICS also set up a development bank, with headquarters in Shanghai headed by an Indian that now has operations in all five countries. The bank approved its first loan to Brazil in April. After coining the acronym BRICS in 2001 Goldman Sachs also sketched out the projected future over the next five decades in a paper entitled 'Dreaming with BRICS' (Wilson and Purushothaman, 2003). The investment bank then upgraded those growth projections in 2011 in light of the BRICS' strong performance over the previous decade. Those projections proved to be mistaken. Of the four economies, only China's GDP has kept pace with the 2011 projections. The others have fallen short by a combined $3 trillion.

A similar disappointment befell BRICS stock market investors. The BRICS equity index compiled by MSCI[2] has lost 75 per cent since its 2009 peak (MSCI, 2020). In October 2015 Goldman Sachs folded one of its BRIC equity funds meant for American investors into a broader emerging-market product. These setbacks seemed to vindicate the curmudgeonly sneer cited by Peter Tasker, of Arcus Investment, dismissing the BRICS as a 'Bloody Ridiculous Investment Concept' (Foxman, 2011).

However, if the BRICS have not sustained the euphoria of 2011, they have amply fulfilled the original 'dream', as articulated by O'Neill in 2001. Even after their recent issues, BRICS' combined GDP ($21 trillion) remains far greater than the Goldman team envisaged back in 2003 ($11.6 trillion) (Dezan Shira & Associates, 2020). Only Russia has failed to live up to those early expectations. China has easily surpassed them. In Brazil growth was slower than Sachs projected but the country's real exchange rate appreciated further than they imagined thereby boosting its GDP in dollar

[2] The MSCI World is a market cap weighted stock market index of 1,652 'world' stocks. It is maintained by MSCI Inc., formerly Morgan Stanley Capital International, and is used as a common benchmark for 'world' or 'global' stock funds.

terms. Moreover, since 2015, when Goldman Sachs closed its fund, the BRICS stock market index has gained almost 20 per cent (MSCI, 2020),

The problem for the BRICS concept could be the size of one of the member countries. Since 2011, China has grown at a faster rate than all the others have. It contributed about half of the club's GDP in 2001 and now accounts for around two-thirds of it (Statista, 2020). China is also home to most of the group's biggest companies. Eight out of the ten largest stocks in the MSCI BRIC index are from China, including Alibaba, Baidu, and Tencent (a tech trio with the acronym, BAT) (MSCI, 2020). As its markets grow and open up to capital inflows China seems destined to become an asset class in its own right. A class that is hard to contain in a 'holistic' emerging-market fund let alone a narrower four-country vehicle. The biggest threat to the BRICS idea may not be the quintet's economic short-comings but the singular success of its largest member.

Mixed Fortunes of the BRICS

BRICS can be broken into two separate groups: those nations that took advantage of globalization's march to integrate themselves into global supply chains (primarily China and India) and those that took advantage of globalization to sell their abundant natural resources (primarily Brazil, Russia and South Africa).

By 2015 China's share of the world's manufacturing output, when measured by value, was roughly 25 per cent. With China's growth in manufacturing prowess, so went China's growth in its middle class. In 1990, China made up nearly 0 per cent of the global middle class, today it comprises 20 per cent (Kharas and Dooley, 2020) with another 350 million people expected to join by 2030 (The World Bank, 2019a; The World Bank, n.d.). India is a similar story but instead of manufacturing, it focused on the services industry. Services account for roughly 50 per cent of India's GDP with a par-ticular emphasis on IT, at $118 billion (Statista, 2020). India is one of the world's leading IT services exporters with the services sector growing 10 per cent from 2015 to 2016 (Statista, 2020). It is no surprise that the rise of India's middle class resembles that of China. Indians went from 1 per cent of the global middle class in 1990 to 28 per cent in 2019, with another 380 million Indians expected to join by 2030 (The World Bank, 2019b).

The collapse in commodity prices has threatened the second group of BRICS nations that rose on the back of their vast natural wealth. Brazil, for example, sells commodities like soya beans, iron ore, and crude oil on global markets. Combining that financial windfall with innovative social programmes helped lift 28.6 million Brazilians from poverty between 2004 and 2014, and in 2016, between 2.5 million and 3.6 million Brazilians fell below the poverty line (Prengaman et al., 2017). As a group, Brazil's poor are arguably the largest beneficiaries of globalization in the Western hemisphere but their status remains volatile. South Africa also used its natural wealth, in this case, rare gems, gold, diamonds, and platinum, to get its economy on track following the dismantling of apartheid. In 1990, the country exported $27 billion in natural resources; by 2019 that number had increased to $43 billion (Workman, 2020). Russia, which spent the 1990s rebuilding itself from the rubble of the Soviet Union, is blessed with abundant energy sources, crude oil, natural gas, metals, and minerals that helped it find its footing. In 2000, 32 per cent of Russians lived below the poverty line, by 2018, just 2.3 per cent did (The World Bank, 2020d). The fall in commodity prices of recent years, however, has done significant damage in all three countries. Brazil's three-year average GDP growth between 2005 and 2007 was 4.41 per cent while the three years ending in 2019 have seen an average growth of 1.29 per cent (The World Bank, 2020a). Over the same time periods, South Africa's growth rate fell from 5.41 per cent to 0.78 per cent (The World Bank, 2020e) and Russia's from 7.69 per cent to 1.9 per cent (The World Bank, 2020c).

Ever Present Corruption

All of these five countries have historically suffered because of corruption with their rising importance in the global economic system putting a spotlight on the issue. Some of the BRICS countries have put significant efforts into fixing the situation and have handled it better than others have. Brazil's spiralling corruption investigations have already taken a toll on former presidents Dilma Rousseff and Michel Temer. Ironically, these same corruption investigations have enhanced the reputation of judicial independence and rule-of-law in Latin America. In South Africa, corruption allegations plagued almost every presidential administration including the current leader Cyril Ramaphosa. In Russia, because of a campaign by opposition activist Alexei Navalny, 47 per cent of Russians now believe 'corruption has significantly taken hold in the Russian government' (Galperovich and Cobus, 2019).

India and China have made bold attempts to combat corruption. Under Prime Minister Narendra Modi, India's government introduced demonetization and did away with 500 and 1,000 rupee notes (86 per cent of the currency in circulation at the time; D'Souza, 2018) in a bid to clamp down on tax evasion and the black market. And while assessment of success has not been great, Modi has become even more ambitious with the introduction of a biometric ID system intended to bypass corruption and fraud by distributing public subsidies and unemployment benefits directly. Despite privacy concerns, more than a billion people have signed up to the scheme (Perrigo, 2018). China's President Xi Jinping is moving forward with a massive multiyear anti-corruption drive, punishing more than 1 million Communist Party officials for corruption offences. This was done both to consolidate power ahead of a major leadership transition and to restore the ruling party's image as the defender of the Chinese people (Agence France-Presse, 2020).

The 'Winners' Remain at Risk

India and China can be labelled as the clear winners among the BRICS nations, but it is not that simple. India and China have the fastest growth rates of any major economies in the world and citizens of these countries remain optimistic about the future. However, nearly two-thirds of Indians remain vulnerable to a slide back into poverty (Roy and Bellman, 2020) and China's economy has slowed as higher wages make manufacturing more expensive. Both countries are especially vulnerable to technological changes that bring automation into the workplace on a larger scale. The World Economic Forum estimates that 30 per cent of the world's jobs will disappear by 2030 (Fleming, 2020).

COVID-19 could catalyse rapid technological innovation and structural change. Nonetheless, the resulting income gains might not be equitably distributed, partly because of the possible effects of innovation on employment. Following technological improvements during 1980–2018, employment declined in 70 per cent of emerging market and developing economies (EMDEs) and 90 per cent of advanced economies (The World Bank, 2020b). The World Bank estimates that 68 per cent of all existing jobs in India are 'at-risk' from automation. In China, the figure is 77 per cent (Chen et al., 2019). Even the sturdiest of the BRICS nations are not as strong as they used to be.

BRICS in the Future

'The BRICS countries will continue to play a key role in the global economy although they reported slower growth in recent years', said Federico Bonaglia, Deputy Director of the Paris-based Organisation for Economic Co-operation and Development (OECD) Development Centre. In a recent interview with Xinhua, Mr Bonaglia said that the slowdown in the growth of the BRICS economies would not have a significant impact on their joint share in the world economy. 'China and India continue to maintain very sustained growth, a situation that both Russia and Brazil are expected to improve next year'. The latest OECD economic outlook expected a return to growth in Brazil and Russia. Meanwhile, China and India are projected to expand their GDP by more than 6 per cent. He noted that India is the only BRICS country that has not experienced a significant slowdown in the past few years with a growth rate of around 8 per cent in 2015 and 5.02 per cent in 2019 (The World Bank, 2019b). The Brazilian economy contracted 3.55

per cent in 2015 but had rebound to 1.14 per cent growth rate in 2019 (The World Bank, 2020a). Russia, which has experienced 'a very complicated situation', will also be able to shake off a growth rate 0.4 per cent in 2019 (The World Bank, 2020c). The outlook for South Africa remains clouded with a growth rate for 2018–19 of 0.63 per cent both years (The World Bank, 2020e).

BRICS economies play an important role by injecting dynamism into the world economy. However, despite this strong progress, the BRICS are facing challenges in terms of productivity growth and innovation. A report commissioned by the New Development Bank and produced by an international group of experts acting as external consultants provides insight into the role of BRICS in the world economy and international development. They cite continued BRICS growth as well as policy initiatives as a substantial benefit to other developing countries and developed countries.

BRICS countries' combined economic weight in 2015 equalled almost a third of the global GDP (or roughly the same as the G7 countries) (Plecher, 2020a). The BRICS are emerging as a new centre of gravity in the international economic system. With the emergence of a multipolar world in which they have become, and are likely to maintain, the central source of economic dynamism, the BRICS countries enjoy a significant position of influence. The BRICS accounted, on average, for an impressive 5.4 per cent of the growth of global GNP during 2008–17 (Parfinenko, 2019). In 2020 the number remains strong for a 4.7 per cent growth by 2023 (Parfinenko, 2019). The BRICS are expected to continue to account for more than a quarter of global economic growth through 2025 (International Monetary Fund, 2020).

The BRICS share of world trade is now approaching 20 per cent, having nearly tripled over the last twenty years. BRICS imports and exports have continued to grow even in a context of shrinking world import and export totals since 2008 (Reddy, 2018). Connectivity among BRICS, between BRICS, other emerging markets, and economically more developing countries (EMDCs) has also increased through enlarged trade and investment. BRICS' contribution to global economic growth through 2030 is expected to be higher if investment rates within BRICS countries increase. Faster

BRICS growth will lead to higher growth rates in all countries, especially EMDCs. Their contribution to world poverty reduction has been sizable. Continued growth remains important for poverty reduction as well as for reducing international inequalities. Activities to promote other global development goals can also be of substantial importance. BRICS development cooperation, and actions to reshape the global economic system so that it is more supportive of EMDCs, can play an important role in expressing the quintet's commitment to international development alongside their role in trade and investment meant to propel economic growth.

BRICS can play an important role in enabling the better provision of global public goods (GPGs), which affect shared economic, social, and environmental conditions. Many underprovided GPGs are of great importance for EMDCs in particular but are of concern to all countries. There is a need for new global governance arrangements that can be more conducive to growth and development. These arrangements include reserve pooling, the strengthening of alternative reserve currencies, new multilateral development banks, and new principles for the governance of sovereign debt, among others. The growing contributions of BRICS to the world economy and the rising importance of the economic relations between them and other EMDCs create an opportunity for new initiatives that would better help to support sustainable and inclusive growth and development. For example, measures to strengthen alternative reserve currencies are made possible by increased economic ties. BRICS can also support pathways for sustainable and inclusive development with conscious and strategic initiatives. They offer a new multilateralism that can help to advance global economic and social development. Cooperation to achieve common goals, both among the BRICS and between the BRICS and others, is likely to be a key feature of international development in the coming decades.

Bibliography

Aenlle, C. de (2013). BRICs, move over: TIMPs are the new emerging market stars. *Reuters*, 28 March.

Agence France-Presse (2020). Former top banker in China pleads guilty to US$12 million corruption after being caught in Xi Jinping's sweep. *South China Morning Post*, 30 July. https://www.scmp.com/news/china/politics/article/3095373/former-top-banker-china-pleads-guilty-us12-million-corruption.

Al-Mohamad, S., Rashid, A., Bakry, W., Jreisat, A., and Vo, X. V. (2020). The impact of BRICS formation on portfolio diversification: Empirical evidence from pre- and post-formation eras. *Cogent Economics & Finance*, 8: 1747890. https://www.tandfonline.com/doi/pdf/10.1080/23322039.2020.1747890.

Chen, H., Li, X., & Frank, M., Qin, X., Xu, W., Cebrian, M., and Rahwan, I. (2019). Automation impacts on China's polarized job market. Research paper.

D'Souza, D. (2018). India demonetization: 99.3% of money returned. *Investopedia*, 29 August. https://www.investopedia.com/news/india-demonetization-993-money-returned/.

Deloitte (2020). The social enterprise at work: Paradox as a path forward. *Deloitte*. https://www2.deloitte.com/us/en/insights/focus/human-capital-trends/2020/technology-and-the-social-enterprise.html.

Dezan Shira & Associates (2020). Calls for BRICS nations to drop US dollar use in intra-bloc transactions. *Dezan Shira & Associates*. https://www.silkroadbriefing.com/news/2020/08/25/calls-for-brics-nations-to-drop-us-dollar-use-in-intra-bloc-transactions/.

Donev, J. M., Afework, B., Hanania, J., and Stenhouse, K. (2020). N11 countries. *Energy Education*. https://energyeducation.ca/encyclopedia/N11_countries.

Exchange Rates (2020). *ExchangeRates.org*, 11 July. https://www.exchangerates.org.uk/USD-RUB-exchange-rate-history.html.

Fleming, S. (2020). A short history of jobs and automation. *World Economic Forum*, 3 September. https://www.weforum.org/agenda/2020/09/short-history-jobs-automation/.

Focus Economics (2020). Economic forecasts from the world's leading economists. *Focus Economics*, 20 October. https://www.focus-economics.com/countries/south-africa.

Foxman, S. (2011). Chart of the day: BRICS = Bloody Ridiculous Investment Concepts. *Business Insider, Australia*, 30 November. https://

www.businessinsider.com/chart-of-the-day-brics--bloody-ridiculous-investment-concepts-2011-11?r=US&IR=T.

Galperovich, D. and Cobus, P. (2019). Navalny 'completely pessimistic' about western curbs on Russian corruption. *Voice of America*, 31 December. https://www.voanews.com/europe/navalny-completely-pessimistic-about-western-curbs-russian-corruption.

International Monetary Fund (2020). World Economic Outlook Database. Washington, DC: IMF. https://www.imf.org/en/Publications/WEO/weo-database/2020/October.

Ionescu, L. (2016). Has China's anti-corruption strategy reduced corruption or purged political rivals? *Contemporary Readings in Law and Social Justice*, 8(1), 245–51.

IPS News (2015). G20 finance ministers committed to sustainable development. *IPS News*, 4 December. http://www.ipsnews.net/2015/09/g20-finance-ministers-committed-to-sustainable-development/.

Kenton, W. (2019). MINTs (Mexico, Indonesia, Nigeria, Turkey). *Investopedia*, 11 September. https://www.investopedia.com/terms/m/mints-mexico-indonesia-nigeria-turkey.asp.

Kharas, H. and Dooley, M. (2020). *China's Influence on the Global Middle Class*. Washington, DC: Brookings Institution.

Manufacturing Output by Country (n.d.). *IMT*. http://news.thomasnet.com/IMT/2013/03/14/china-widens-lead-as-worlds-largest-manufacturer/.

MSCI (2020). MSCI BRIC Index. *MSCI.com*, 30 October. https://www.msci.com/documents/10199/3653ff70-93d4-4e88-9c4e-70d8efb10923#:~:text='The%20MSCI%20BRIC%20Index%20is,%2C%20Russia%2C%20India%20and%20China.

Musacchio, A. and Werker, E. (2016). Mapping frontier economies. *Harvard Business Review*, December.

O'Neill, J. (2001). *Building Better Global Economic BRICs*. Global Economics Paper No. 66. New York: Goldman Sachs.

Parfinenko, T. (2019). International economic integration of BRICS countries: Driver of regional and global economic growth. *Advances in Economics, Business and Management Research*, 131, 426–31.

Perrigo, B. (2018). India has been collecting eye scans and fingerprint records from every citizen: Here's what to know. *Time*, 28 September.

Plecher, H. (2020a). Global gross domestic product (GDP) 2021. *Statista*, 3 June. https://www.statista.com/statistics/268750/global-gross-domestic-product-gdp/.

Plecher, H. (2020b). Total population of the BRIC countries from 2014 to 2024. *Statista*, 2 June. https://www.statista.com/statistics/254205/total-population-of-the-bric-countries/.

Prengaman, P., DiLorenzo, S., and Trielli, D. (2017). Millions return to poverty in Brazil, ending 'boom' decade. *AP News*, 23 October.

Rasoulinezhad, E. and Jabalameli, F. (2018). Do BRICS countries have similar trade integration patterns? *Journal of Economic Integration*, 33(1), 1011–45.

Reddy, S. (2018). The growing BRICS economies: An INET series. *The Institute for New Economic Thinking*, 12 April. https://www.ineteconomics.org/perspectives/blog/the-growing-brics-economies-an-inet-series#:~:text=The%20BRICS%20share%20of%20world,and%20export%20totals%20since%202008.

Reed, S. (2017). The BRICS and a changing world. *Developing Economics*, 27 September. https://developingeconomics.org/2017/09/27/the-brics-and-a-changing-world/#:~:text=The%20BRICS%20accounted%2C%20on%20average,over%20the%20last%20twenty%20years.

Roy, R. and Bellman, E. B. (2020). India to spend $22.5 billion to help poor survive coronavirus shutdown. *The Wall Street Journal*, 26 March.

Statista (2020). Gross domestic product (GDP) of the BRIC countries from 2009 to 2021. *Statista/Economy & Politics—International*, 2 June. https://www.statista.com/statistics/254281/gdp-of-the-bric-countries/.

Tett, G. (2010). The story of the BRICs. *Financial Times*, 15 January.

The Global Economy (2020). Countries. *The Global Economy.com.* https://www.theglobaleconomy.com/economies/.

The World Bank (2019a). *China—Data.* The World Bank Data Bank—China. https://data.worldbank.org/country/CN.

The World Bank (2019b). *India—Data.* The World Bank Data Bank—India. http://data.worldbank.org/country/india.

The World Bank (2020a). *Brazil GDP Growth Rate 1961–2020.* Washington, DC: The World Bank.

The World Bank (2020b). *Global Productivity: Trends, Drivers, and Policies.* Washington, DC: The World Bank.

The World Bank (2020c). *Russia GDP Growth Rate 1990–2020*. Washington, DC: The World Bank.

The World Bank (2020d). *Russian Poverty Rate 1993–2020*. Washington, DC: The World Bank.

The World Bank (2020e). *South Africa GDP Growth Rate 1961–2020*. Washington, DC: The World Bank.

The World Bank (n.d.). Russian Federation statistics. Washington, DC: The World Bank. https://data.worldbank.org/country/russian-federation.

Timmons, H. (2015). The BRICs era is over, even at Goldman Sachs. *Quartz*, 9 November.

Wilson, D. and Purushothaman, R. (2003). *Dreaming with BRICS: The Path to 2050*. Global Economics Paper No. 99. New York: Goldman Sachs.

Workman, D. (2020). South Africa's Top 10 Exports. *World's Top Exports*. http://www.worldstopexports.com/south-africas-top-10-exports/.

3
Rising Stars, Hot Markets, and Brave New Worlds

As the investor focus on the BRICS markets has continued to evolve, similar definitional criteria have been applied to other countries and regions. As a result, other emerging investment 'clusters' are being defined. This chapter looks at some of these groups and, with input from academicians, practitioners, and practical thinkers, sorts out what common factors add to their attraction, problems, and potential. These emerging economies are grouped as TIMP (Turkey, Indonesia, Mexico, and Philippines), MINT (Mexico, Indonesia, Nigeria, and Turkey), Next-11 or N11 (Bangladesh, Egypt, Indonesia, Iran, Mexico, Nigeria, Pakistan, the Philippines, Turkey, South Korea, and Vietnam), and Frontier Markets (MSCI Inc., 2020)[1] We examine the critical nature of existing positives and negatives that impact or impede growth and how they are being addressed. Observation on infrastructure and demographics, financial system status, governance and governments, are compared with criteria generally present in developing economies such as stability of the countries, politics, and fiscal and monetary policy. The chapter also examines other factors like trade barriers, regulatory environments, access to equitable quality, education, geographic location advantage, and other factors that may be indicators of future emergence onto the global stage.

Initially, we will examine what most of these countries have in common. Most of them have similar infrastructure and demographics.

---

[1] Frontier Markets countries include: Bahrain, Bangladesh, Burkina Faso, Benin, Croatia, Estonia, Guinea-Bissau, Ivory Coast, Jordan, Kenya, Kuwait, Lebanon, Lithuania, Kazakhstan, Mauritius, Mali, Morocco, Niger, Nigeria, Oman, Romania, Serbia, Senegal, Slovenia, Sri Lanka, Togo, Tunisia, and Vietnam.

Global Business in the Age of Transformation. Mahesh K. Joshi and J.R. Klein, Oxford University Press.
© Mahesh K. Joshi and J.R. Klein 2021. DOI: 10.1093/oso/9780192847232.003.0003

They all have a relatively young population, high ratios of workers to retirees, a basic lack of infrastructure with potential for growth, banking systems that are under leveraged, and credit is generally well controlled with little overextension of either individuals or governments. Demographics in all of these countries are attractive as compared to other countries in emerging markets. Other, not so attractive common features are corruption, regulatory barriers, and unstable governance. Transparency International (Transparency International, 2019), in its annual reports, includes a corruption index that scores countries around the world. Whether surprising or not, one thing many of these emerging markets have in common is the remarkably high degree of corruption. These issues impact the growth potential and are a cause for a weak future.

Rising Stars

Using data from the World Bank in combination with their data, Goldman Sachs published the 2050 report (Goldman Sachs, 2003) in which they examined basic gross domestic product (GDP) and purchasing power parity (PPP) to reflect on their attraction, problems, and potential. The report presented growth profiles in GDP and PPP emerging economies including the TIMP and MINT. In 2012, the highest-ranking GDP although MINT was Mexico. According to the World Bank economy ranking in 2018, Mexico dropped to 15th, Indonesia maintained its 16th position, Nigeria moved up the rank to 31st, and Turkey stood at 18th position. Meanwhile, the same document projected that by the year 2023, all the four MINT countries will be among the first 20 world economies, with Mexico at 15th, Indonesia at 16th, Nigeria at 20th, and Turkey at 17th positions (The World Bank Group, 2021). It points out that larger emerging economies like the BRIC nations will grow much larger and will all be in the top six with China at number one, India at number three, Brazil at number five and Russia at number six. Also, other similar reports have speculated on the ten top economies by 2050. They speculate that China, India, and the United States will probably be one, two, and three, but Japan, Germany, and the United Kingdom be eight, nine, and ten with France falling from the list (PwC Global, 2017).

It should also be noted that each group designation, e.g. TIMP, MINT, etc., may include the same country. Turkey, for example, ends up in TIMP, MINT, and N11. This is a result of the nomenclature designed primarily by investment firms that recognize the same indicators but may expand or contract inclusion in a group based on their investment criteria. For this reason, we will primarily focus on individual countries as members of a particular group rather than the group itself.

Turkey

A list of Turkey's advantages must begin with its geographic location. It is a natural bridge between Asia and Europe. It has a $761.8 billion economy (The World Bank, 2020a) with 2.8 per cent growth and a per capita income of $28,455 (OECD, 2020). By comparison, China, with the second-largest global economy has a per capita income around $8,254 (Trading Economics, 2020). Some cities like Shanghai and Beijing have per capita income of $20,000 (Statista, 2020b). The idea here is that Turkey's starting point for growth is already pretty high. Secondly, Turkey has had some foreign direct investment (FDI) inflow, although not as much as some larger countries, but has seen a decline from $60 billion to $8.4 billion in 2019. Overall the economy's macroeconomic stability has suffered in the last several years. The slowdown was due to global economic uncertainty as well as weak economic growth (Nordea, 2020). There has been political turmoil but overall, it has been a fairly stable country. Fiscal policy has been fairly prudent with budget deficits and public debt kept under control. Of late the country has experienced some inflationary pressures, but the financial sector has remained stable and competitive. It does have its challenges, however. Political turmoil, the lack of transparency in government, and instability in the rule of law have been negative elements especially in terms of attracting foreign investment. That fact is critical to the development of many emerging countries. Turkey is a secular republic. Former President Erdogan's party pushed a somewhat

Islamist agenda, potentially eroding Turkey's Euro-Atlantic relations by cracking down on freedom of speech and the media. Turkey has been a member of NATO since 1952 and the EU has granted them country candidate status. It has fairly competitive tax rates with a top personal tax rate of 40 per cent and a top corporate tax rate of 22 per cent (Deloitte, 2020). Regulations remain a drag on entrepreneurship, which limits the emergence of a more dynamic economy. Trade is important to Turkey and given its geographic location is a huge economic driver. More than 61 per cent of the country's GDP is in exports and imports (The Global Economy, 2019b, 2019c). Turkey has been trying to attract foreign investments and to prioritize publicly owned corporations and enterprises. Banking is stable, well-capitalized, and resilient. The presence of foreign banks is not as much as would be expected of an economy sitting on the border of Europe and Asia (The World Bank, 2019b).

Indonesia

Indonesia has one of the world's largest populations with 274.6 million people (WorldOmeter, 2020a). It is the fourth largest country in the world (WorldOmeter, 2020a). Its GDP is growing and as income levels rise, so do the numbers of middle class. Indonesia had a 2019 GDP of $1.1 trillion and a PPP of $9,980 with a growth rate of 5.0 per cent (IMF, 2020). Even in comparison to its larger competitors—India, China, and the United States—these numbers are impressive. Indonesia, however, does have its shortcomings. To show that it is not all about the numbers, Indonesia has still not reached the global stage. In terms of infrastructure and institutional development, Indonesia is not close to the developed world. The country lacks a well-functioning legal and regulatory framework, there is rampant corruption, a slow justice system, and uncertainty about rules and regulations. These shortcomings continue to undercut the momentum towards a more dynamic economic environment that is of paramount importance for the growth of the private sector and the attraction of foreign investment. All emerging nations indeed face similar institutional challenges. They share issues of captive markets, alienated labour, unreliable regulations, and ambiguous policies. Indonesia has yet to find the will to begin to address systemic change.

It does, however, have a unique advantage. Indonesia is a member of G20, an informal group of 19 countries and the European Union with representatives of the International Monetary Fund and the World Bank. In addition, the country is an important driving force within the Association of Southeast Asian Nations (ASEAN), and is attempting to play a greater role at that level which is a positive indicator. Indonesia's practice of governance in terms of freedom for people, property rights, and regulatory environment is generally respected. Another potential positive indicator is the emergence of signs of independence in the judiciary. There is one overwhelming concern, outside of the list of institutional issues, and that is the problem of corruption. However, the World Economic Forum's global competitive index report (World Economic Forum, 2017), in its indicator of anti-corruption efforts, states that Indonesia's efforts may be starting to pay off and improving on measures related to ethics. While the impact of stabilization in the regulatory environment remains weak, it shows improvement and a positive trajectory. The International Monetary Fund praised the fuel subsidy reform the government implemented and cited it as a potential model for other countries. Indonesia's energy subsidies are provided directly to and only to poorer consumers with indications of minimal misuse.

As we examine Indonesian global growth numbers we recognize that the country's remaining challenges stem from leadership and infrastructure issues. When reform thinking gains acceptance, structural adjustment will start, corruption will be dealt with, and the public finance environment will improve. Along with its advantage of numbers, these innovations could drive growth and earn Indonesia a place on the global stage.

Mexico

With a population of 129 million (WorldOmeter, 2020b), a $10,276 GDP per capita, a PPP of $2.3 trillion, and proximity to one of the largest economies in the world, the United States, Mexico, like Turkey, has a favourable starting point for growth (Global Edge, 2018). Its geography and natural resources are attractive to global trade. It has benefited from the North American Free Trade Agreement (NAFTA) and has seen a lot of investments in the manufacturing sector and has started to upscale and improve competencies in that sector. Driven by NAFTA, the auto, aviation, aerospace, and local domestic demand has grown. Mexico's large economy has benefited from its proximity to the United States and has seen FDI of $9.5 billion, representing 2.3 per cent of GDP (The Global Economy, 2019a) and has enjoyed good access to resources in North America. As of 1 July 2020, a new agreement replaced NAFTA, the US–Mexico–Canada Agreement (USMCA). As this new agreement begins to play out it may result in some adverse risk; however, Mexico has a lot of free trade agreements with several countries outside of the United States. If USMCA was to have a negative impact on trade between the United States and Mexico its geography with access to Atlantic and Pacific trade routes would most likely still see companies investing in Mexico and continuing robust trade around the world. Fiscal and monetary policies have helped them manage their macroeconomic performances. Structural reforms in energy and telecommunication sectors and a robust state-owned oil company have resulted in solid economic strength. Also, reform and revision of commercial operations have become more streamlined and facilitated business operations and start-ups. Trade is an important part of the Mexican economy with the combined value of imports and exports making up 80 per cent of its GDP (The World Bank, 2018). It also has a competitive banking system and an open financial sector. The banking system is relatively well capitalized, has a healthy amount of foreign participation, and is growing.

As with all emerging countries Mexico has some shortcomings. The judicial, institutional, and regulatory systems are still weak with corruption and high levels of crime remaining issues. The government has taken actions to bring about reform but there are still abundant opportunities to do more. If there is a concerted effort from a governance and infrastructure reform agenda the Mexican economy could stand in a good place to play on the international stage.

Philippines

The Philippines is a relatively small country located in Asia with a population of 106.7 million (The World Bank, 2020b). One of its biggest advantages is that English is one of its official languages. English-speaking workers have spawned the whole call centre industry that came about when firms outsourced direct customer service in operations to countries like India. The pushback from customers about customer service out of India was their discomfort with local accents. This opened an opportunity for the Philippines where English speaking talent is typically more Westernized. This sector is also competitive from its low cost of service.

Though it is a smaller economy, the Philippines occupies a niche which is conducive to growth. As part of Asia, it benefits from the aggressive strategies of its neighbours. The Philippines' GDP is $360 billion with an expected 2022 growth rate of 6.0 per cent. Inflation is nominal with an unemployment rate of 9.96 per cent (The Global Economy, 2019a). The GDP per capita is $3,338 and PPP is $8,908 (The World Bank, 2019a). That is comparable to some of the other countries in our list and so overall the Philippines is well placed. Agriculture is still a significant part of the economy with some industrial production in areas of electronics, apparel, and shipbuilding, with customer services call centres still growing. The Philippines also receives large inward capital remittances from overseas most of it due to the cross-border Filipino workforce. The amounts to a staggering 10 per cent of the country's GDP (The World Bank, 2019a).

The Philippines has a pressing need for institutional reforms in areas such as business freedom, investment freedom, rule of law, and governance. Regulatory, statutory, and social reform is needed in the areas of property rights, corruption and cronyism, and the issue of wealth and income inequity, with a disproportionate level of assets and political power in the hands of a few controlling families, needs to be addressed. A culture of impunity has been reinforced by recent leadership. There is little incentive for economic activity other than sustenance in a system that dampens entrepreneurship. Entrepreneurship is the key to the Philippines' long-term economic success. The Philippines needs to legislate reforms that will improve the overall environment for entrepreneurship and the development of a robust private sector that will be conducive for an internal workforce to promote growth. This along with its relatively stable financial sector could expand the Philippines' emerging status.

Nigeria

With its abundance of natural resources, Nigeria is truly a fuel-based economy. It is a country awash with paradox. With a population of 186 million, it uses about the same amount of energy as the 66.5 million population of the UK. Almost every business has to generate its power at substantial costs. Yet the country has been growing at a rate of 2.1 per cent. Its GDP is $448 billion and PPP is $5,135 (The Global Economy, 2019a) which puts it at the low end of the emerging world. While the country's parochial history has yet to transition to current realities, in 2015, for the first time, it experienced a peaceful transfer of power. While this is not uncommon on the African continent, one of Nigeria's critical issues is the instability of the entire region. As a result, it has been marred with not just corruption but the issue of guaranteeing the personal safety of companies, domestic and foreign, operating in the country. It struggles with the issue of insurgencies and terrorist groups and security threats that negatively impact poverty and unemployment which exacerbates the lack of transparency in the economic system. It enjoys an abundance of natural resources, specifically oil and gas, but its heavy over-dependence on oil—which accounts for 90 per cent of export earnings—exposes the economy to major risks of price volatility as experienced in the current environment (Statista, 2020a).

There are some positive indicators with the judiciary system becoming a bit more independent in the face of political indifference, corruption, and lack of funding. For Nigeria oil and gas is literally the economy with most of the labour force working in the sector. As has been noted in other emerging markets, the country needs to feed economic stability and it needs to develop a robust private sector. Those efforts must be led by the government or supported by the government with diverse initiatives incentivizing entrepreneurship and private sector development. It must work to diversify away from a sole-sourced oil and gas economy. This will lead to more foreign direct investment and impact the judiciary and regulatory systems thus making the country more attractive. Investors have added Nigeria to the MINT group based on its potential for stability and investment. Successful accomplishment of those expectations will depend on Nigeria's handling of its internal challenges.

Hot Markets

Goldman Sachs identified the N11 countries (Bangladesh, Egypt, Indonesia, Iran, Mexico, Nigeria, Pakistan, the Philippines, Turkey, South Korea, and Vietnam) in 2005 (Goldman Sachs, 2007). They were tagged as the next in line to become economic powerhouses. The main criteria used in this assessment were the stability of the countries, politics, and fiscal and monetary policy. Other factors considered were the number of trade barriers imposed by the country and the quality of education. All of the N11 countries passed these tests in varying degrees. The open debate is whether these eleven countries will one day become as influential as the BRICS, most particularly in the investment sector. Will they over time grow to have a significant place in worldwide GDP? Will their size and differences in character lead to internal and external cooperation as happened with the BRICS nations?

Dr Nikhil Celly, strategy and international business professor at C. T. Bauer College of Business at the University of Houston, Texas, observes that general evaluation of countries is based on similar characteristics. Indicators like macroeconomic stability such as government deficit, external debt, balance of payments, and inflation are baseline elements. Other essential components include how open are the country's investment conditions and current investment rates are viewed by investors. A critical evaluative factor is the country's political conditions, which can be a primary risk because of potential volatility. The market must be stable as a destination to be conducive for investment and business activity. This entails an examination of investment and macro stability such as political stability, rule of law, and things like governance, regulations, corruption, and legal conditions. Internally, evaluation looks at the history of how the country's governance, fiscal, legal, regulatory, and social institutions have developed. Long-term growth factors such as human capital, education, quality of institutions, life expectancy, and the age of the population are also taken into consideration. A younger population indicates a potentially sustainable workforce with skills and ability over an extended period. Finally, there should be a determination of the status and capacity of infrastructure and technological status. Transportation, shipping, and communication are important for potential growth, as is the digital infrastructure. How prevalent are the Internet, mobile technology and the basic acceptance of computers and other digital forms of communication and technology?

Jim O'Neill, the Chair of Goldman Sachs Asset Management Group, coined the acronym BRIC as well as N11. He observed that the common factor for N11 is a large, young, growing population. N11 represents almost 19 per cent of the world population (Goldman Sachs, 2007). The age of the workforce can lead to stability in the long term with the growth in population creating a significant consumer base with internal and external impact. He also cites the attraction of diversity. This is not the diversity of gender or culture but is economic diversity. N11 includes developed countries like South Korea and Mexico with their relatively stable and sustainable economies and at the other end of the spectrum Bangladesh and Pakistan with potential for but not visible stability. The developed countries add stability to the mix while the undeveloped ones add potential growth. The young, growing population is the key. If stability can be achieved in the less impactful economies, they could see high investor return, growth in consumer spending, and potential for workforce productivity that move them solidly into emerging status. O'Neill believes that the fifteen countries that make up BRIC and N11 will generate an additional $10 to $20 trillion for the global economy in the next decade (Goldman Sachs, 2007).

Today's comparison between BRICS and N11 highlights their position and potential impact on world markets. BRICS has some diversity but is distinguished by its common ground in large populations. They are more similar in their stages of development with some members, like China, after experiencing dramatic growth, showing signs of maturity with low but still impressive rates. N11 countries have wider differences in industries with a more diverse range of industries. While the smaller countries like Pakistan and Bangladesh rely on a limited number of specific industries, countries like Mexico with tourism, manufacturing, and a large domestic market are more diverse. Industrial diversity in the N11 is much greater than the BRICS. Other important differences in N11 are living standards, differences in income, education, and law. South Korea, for example, is a high-income country and in some thinking could be classified as a developed country. South Korea has long been considered one of the four Asian Tigers along with Hong Kong, Taiwan and Singapore.

In addition to the economic differences, we also see differences in foreign policy and relationships with other countries. As an example, Iran with its positives of huge oil reserves and a noteworthy labour force with observable worldwide expertise in engineering and technology skills has shown muted growth. Because its authoritarian leadership has stifled economic growth and imposed price controls and subsidies for many inefficient industries the country has traditionally been closed to the Western world. This position has led to sanctions, particularly on its oil exports, which is a significant part of the economy. There are some subtle positive indicators, however. The country has worked well with its neighbour Turkey on pipeline projects to connect Iran's oil and gas fields to Turkey and then to the European markets. Iran's huge potential remains constrained.

History has shown us that it is harder for the N11 countries to come together on a playing field of cooperation than it is for the BRICS nations. Part of that is due to their differences in geography.

From the Middle East to Southeast Asia the variations of religion, ideology, local politics, and trade make growth more problematic. The biggest variance between N11 and BRICS is their agreement on a common goal. In the BRICS, this was made easier as a result of their large populations which meant that growth was a natural consequence. Big populations have more people to produce goods and services and to purchase products. The N11 grouping also has a sizeable population but unlike BRICS they see no immediate need to form a BRICS kind of union to influence the global economy.

N11 can be divided into three kinds of groups. The first group are countries that have a fairly well-developed economy like South Korea, Mexico, Turkey, and also Indonesia. They present a level of stability, economic strength, and technical infrastructure making them attractive for foreign investment and trade. The second group is countries on the cusp. Countries like Pakistan or the Philippines and Vietnam have a marked potential for emergence into strongly developed economies. Vietnam, for example, has shown signs of emergence with some political stability and economic reform. The third group are the countries to watch. Nations like Iran, Egypt, and Nigeria with tremendous potential in resource reserves and work-force strength and sustainability remain plagued with political issues both internal and external. Bangladesh fits into this group not because of its political issues but simply because of its low level of development in general.

The N11 discussion is all about picking winners and losers. Countries that are more stable politically whether through democracy, authoritarian, one-party rule, or dictatorship, will have better prospects for consistent growth. Investors are looking for stability and continuity of policies and regulations. In the N11 not just population but growth rates have been comparable to those of Western or Southeast Asian developed economies. For businesses, large populations and high growth rates mean that these will expand rapidly providing even more potential customers. Sustained economic growth creates new consumer markets. However, there are differences in the levels of growth within the group; therefore, some of the countries especially those with higher growth will simply be more profitable for certain businesses. Finally, relying on an examination of the past to drive expansion to these markets may not be sufficient. These countries have pretty unique internal and external environments for businesses to consider. These differences need to be linked directly to corporations' long-term strategy and be customized for individual countries. Any expansion to N11 needs to involve a lot of customization to be successful.

Brave New World

The categorization of countries into Frontier Markets was a function of investor diligence as to the potential for growth, stability, and return. The term Frontier Market was coined in 1992 by Farida Khambata of the International Finance Corporation and it is referred to as a subset of emerging markets. Subsequent to that, frontier indexes were established by major providers like Standard and Poor's,[2] MSCI,[3] Russell Investments,[4] and FTSE.[5] The number of Frontier Markets in these industries ranges from thirty-seven countries in the MSCI index to forty-one in the Russell frontier index. These markets are generally concentrated in Eastern Europe, Africa, the Middle East, South America, and Asia. The biggest markets are in Kuwait, Qatar, the United Arab Emirates, Nigeria, Argentina, and Kazakhstan. Initially, the criterion for inclusion in the group was that the country was not a component of any emerging market or developed market indices. Other qualifications were its economic development status, market access ability, liquidity, and foreign investment restrictions.

---

[2] Standard & Poor's Financial Services LLC (S&P) is an American financial services company. It is a division of S&P Global that publishes financial research and analysis on stocks, bonds, and commodities.

[3] MSCI Inc. (formerly Morgan Stanley Capital International and MSCI Barra), is an American provider of equity, fixed income, hedge fund stock market indexes, and equity portfolio analysis tools.

[4] Russell Investments is a global asset management firm, founded in 1936. It provides multi-asset investing solutions to institutional investors, as well as to individuals via financial advisers.

[5] The Financial Times Stock Exchange 100 Index, also called the FTSE 100 Index, FTSE 100, FTSE, or, informally, the 'Footsie', is a share index of the 100 companies listed on the London Stock Exchange with the highest market capitalization.

As with our other conversations regarding emerging markets we begin with the question 'Are the Frontier Markets a real growth opportunity for businesses?' These markets are often found at an early stage of development and this is the main factor in why they get people's attention. In the investment world, they can provide an opportunity to diversify the portfolio risk with both upside and downside potential. The diversity offers not only risk but also good growth potential, which translates to return. Early movers in an asset class such as Frontier Markets believe that there is potential for the group to become a significant portion of the global equity market. The Frontier Markets of the past have become the major economies of today. China in 1980 was considered a Frontier Market and has grown to the second-largest economy in the world. The countries on the list of Frontier Markets may not even have existed a few decades ago. Technology will allow frontier countries to move much faster than we have seen in the past and with that advantage and connectivity to global stock markets may drive Frontier Market growth to be even faster. Financial markets are opening up and if this trend continues, the Frontier Markets of today have a good chance of becoming the developed markets of the future. There is also a risk of reverse migration as has happened in Argentina and Venezuela where the inability to address basic elements of the economy, such as single resource reliance has caused the economy to regress. As an example, Kuwait is wealthy and generally well developed but relies on energy for almost 92 per cent of its revenues (Organization of the Petroleum Exporting Countries, 2019). With the noted differences in the number of nations included in various groups, it is evident that the criteria differ and are by no means rigid. The biggest Frontier Markets are Kuwait, Qatar, and the UAE. They are all wealthy and well developed. Their infrastructure is well established and, in some places, put developed countries to shame. However, from the standpoint of criteria characteristics such as liquidity of capital, a lot of businesses remain state-owned, but they have still been captured in the categorization.

Why are Frontier Markets getting the attention? From an investment perspective, they represent a real growth opportunity other than just purely finance-driven. First, the growth potential based on the demographics of many of these countries is a population of around 3 billion (Business Insider, 2020). This is bigger than any emerging country and bigger than the developed countries with nearly 40 per cent of the world population (Business Insider, 2020). The population is relatively young with a collective 60 per cent under thirty years of age (T. Rowe Price, 2020). This is even more significant when countries like Japan and others have ageing populations. They are also attractive because they currently account for only 5 per cent of the world's nominal GDP and only 0.4% of global market capitalization (Hussain, 2020). The nominal GDP is a function of population size while market capitalization indicates undeveloped economic infrastructure to support growth even though some of the countries are rich and developed in terms of the market. The average labour costs are low compared with costs in other nations and with the demographic advantage and a nominal GDP, there are significantly good long-term growth prospects. In 2011 for instance, Frontier Markets had an average GDP growth of 4.9 per cent, which is almost three times faster than the 1.6 per cent average for the ten largest advanced economies according to the World Bank (J.P. Morgan, 2015).

Most of the developed and even emerging countries are globally linked with increased global economic integration. Frontier Markets, however, have a lower degree of correlation with the global economy. This could be an effective edge when considering portfolio diversification. In times of recession or accelerating growth, their exposure would be measured making them a useful diversification mechanism. When comparing the average frontier economy over time frontiers are outpacing their larger counterparts with GDP per capita growth up around 40 per cent since 2013 (Quisenberry, 2018). There are volatility and wide ranges from year to year. For patient investors with a long-term horizon and potential for significant returns, such markets may be attractive.

The potential related risks are associated with liquidity. In countries with poor financial and banking systems or an abundance of state-owned industries or institutions changing asset classes could be a problem. Associated with that are the political and geopolitical risks. Nations that are located in unstable areas with volatile environments can be an issue. Also, the policies of governments and governance itself can change quickly. Another risk is inflation. Inflation is a constant threat in some of these countries and if not controlled can quickly result in return impairment. These issues along with things like the lack of transparency and availability or manipulation of information can impact growth. Frontier Markets offer investors advantages of above average returns with their favourable demographics, taking into account the opportunity for portfolio diversification and risks in the current state of development. As the last investment frontier of investing there is a role for select investors.

Twenty years ago, emerging markets were undergoing similar developments as Frontier Markets today. Frontier Markets are generally less researched than emerging market peers, and attract less investment. However, many companies are well-positioned to benefit from the next wave of economic development. Frontier Markets with attractive demographics offer great exposure to domestic demand and some of the fastest-growing economies.

Bibliography

Business Insider (2020). Frontier market investing strategy. *Business Insider*, 24 April. https://www.businessinsider.com/frontier-market-investing-recommendation-strategy-from-manny-stotz-howard-marks-2020-4.

Citywire (2020). Hidden growth: 'Forgotten 40' frontier markets flash recovery signs. *Citywire*, 21 October. https://citywire.co.uk/investment-trust-insider/news/hidden-growth-forgotten-40-frontier-markets-flash-recovery-signs/a1415455.

Deloitte (2020). International tax, Turkey highlights 2020. *Deloitte*, January. https://www2.deloitte.com/content/dam/Deloitte/global/Documents/Tax/dttl-tax-turkeyhighlights-2020.pdf.

Global Edge (2018). Mexico: Economy. *Global Edge*. https://globaledge.msu.edu/countries/mexico/economy.

Goldman Sachs (2003). *Dreaming with BRICs: The Path to 2050*. New York: Goldman Sachs.

Goldman Sachs (2007). *Beyond the BRICs: A Look at the 'Next 11'*. New York: Goldman Sachs.

Hussain, M. A (2020). Commentary: ESG investing—expanding the universe to new frontiers. *Pensions & Investments*, 28 April. https://www.pionline.com/industry-voices/commentary-esg-investing-expanding-universe-new-frontiers.

International Monetary Fund (2020). World Economic Outlook Database. Washington, DC: IMF. https://www.imf.org/en/Publications/WEO/weo-database/2020/October.

J.P. Morgan (2015). *Frontier Markets: The New Emerging Markets*. New York: J.P. Morgan.

MSCI Inc (2020). *MSCI Frontier Markets Index (USD)*. New York: MSCI Inc.

Nordea (2020). Turkey: Investing in Turkey. *Nordea*. https://www.nordeatrade.com/fi/explore-new-market/turkey/investment.

OECD (2020). Country statistical profile: Turkey 2020/1. In *Country Statistical Profiles: Key Tables from OECD*. Paris: OECD. https://doi.org/10.1787/g2g9ead4-en.

Organization of the Petroleum Exporting Countries (2019). Kuwait facts and figures. Vienna: OPEC. https://www.opec.org/opec_web/en/about_us/165.htm.

PwC Global (2017). The World in 2050, the long view: How will the global economic order change by 2050? *PwC Global*, February. https://www.pwc.com/gx/en/research-insights/economy/the-world-in-2050.html.

Quisenberry, C. (2018). Frontier markets: A comparative analysis. *Investments & Wealth Monitor*, November/December. https://investmentsandwealth.org/getattachment/10f6792b-8916-43a9-85ef-ec7298662e8a/IWM18NovDec-FrontierMarkets.pdf.

Statista (2020a). Contribution of oil sector to GDP in Nigeria 2018–2020. *Statista*, 31 August. https://www.statista.com/statistics/1165865/contribution-of-oil-sector-to-gdp-in-nigeria/.

Statista (2020b). Gross domestic product (GDP) of Shanghai municipality in China from 2010 to 2019. *Statista*, 12 November. https://www.statista.com/statistics/802355/china-gdp-of-shanghai/#:~:text=Per%20capita%20GDP%20of%20Shanghai,the%20average%20in%20East%20Asia.

T. Rowe Price (2020). Frontier Markets Equity Fund. *T. Rowe Price*, 31 October. https://www.troweprice.com/financial-intermediary/pt/en/funds/sicav/frontier-markets-equity-fund.html.

The Global Economy (2019a). The global economy. *The Global Economy.com*. https://www.theglobaleconomy.com/Mexico/Foreign_Direct_Investment/ #:~:text=%3A%20For%20that%20indicator%2C%20we%20 provide,from%202019%20is%202.3%20percent.

The Global Economy (2019b). Turkey: Exports, percent of GDP. *The Global Economy.com*. https://www.theglobaleconomy.com/Turkey/exports/.

The Global Economy (2019c). Turkey: Imports, percent of GDP. *The Global Economy.com*. https://www.theglobaleconomy.com/Turkey/imports/.

The World Bank (2018). Mexico trade statistics: Exports, imports, products, tariffs, GDP and related Development Indicator. *World Integrated Trade Solution*. https://wits.worldbank.org/CountryProfile/en/MEX#:~:text= Mexico%20All%20Products%20Exports%20and%20Imports&text= Mexico%20services%20export%20is%2028%2C767%2C605%2C127, percentage%20of%20GDP%20is%2041.16%25.

The World Bank (2019a). Philippines GDP per capita. *Trading Economics*. https://tradingeconomics.com/philippines/gdp-per-capita#:~:text= GDP%20per%20capita%20in%20Philippines%20is%20expected%20 to%20reach%203000.00,according%20to%20our%20econometric%20 models.

The World Bank (2019b). *The World Bank DataBank—Demographics*. Washington, DC: The World Bank.

The World Bank (2020a). *The World Bank in Turkey*, 19 October. Washington, DC: The World Bank. https://www.worldbank.org/en/ country/turkey/overview.

The World Bank (2020b). *World Development Indicators*. Washington, DC: The World Bank. https://datatopics.worldbank.org/world-development-indicators/.

The World Bank Group (2021). *Global Economic Prospects*. World Bank Group Flagship Report. Washington, DC: The World Bank Group.

Trading Economics (2020). China GDP per capita. *Trading Economics*. https://tradingeconomics.com/china/gdp-per-capita#:~:text=GDP %20per%20capita%20in%20China%20is%20expected%20to%20 reach%208130.00,according%20to%20our%20econometric%20 models.

Transparency International (2019). *Corruption Perceptions Index*. Berlin: Transparency International. https://www.transparency.org/en/cpi/2019/ results.

World Economic Forum (2017). *2017–2018 WEF Global Competitiveness Index (GCI) results.* Brand South Africa, 9 October. https://www.brand-southafrica.com/resources-downloads/knowledge-hub/2017-2018-wef-global-competitiveness-index-gci-results.

WorldOmeter (2020a). Indonesia population. *WorldOmeter.* https://www.worldometers.info/world-population/indonesia-population/.

WorldOmeter (2020b). Mexico population. *WorldOmeter.* https://www.worldometers.info/world-population/mexico-population/#:~:text=Mexico%202020%20population%20is%20estimated,(and%20dependencies)%20by%20population.

4

Regulating Global Commerce

Over the last half-century, the number of countries in the world has increased from 89 (Travel Independent, 2016) in 1950 to 195 in 2020 (WorldOmeter, 2020). Technology has driven increases in the speed of business, global connectivity, and complexity. In this environment, it is no wonder that regulatory systems are challenged. The World Trade Organization (WTO), World Bank, and the International Monetary Fund (IMF) were created to establish a framework for economic cooperation and development with the central theme of creating a stable and prosperous global economy. The goals of these organizations remain the same but their work is constantly changing. The WTO is the only international organization dealing with global rules of trade between nations. The World Bank promotes long-term economic development. It works on poverty eradication and provides technical and financial support and policy reforms by implementing specific projects. The IMF was created to promote international monetary cooperation, to provide policy advice, and carry out capacity development to help countries build and maintain strong economies. The technologically driven disruption in economic models, the emergence of developing economies, and changing financial systems present an evolutionary environment that requires challenging solutions. The question for consideration is, 'are the world's regulators up to the challenge?'

In 1945 at the United Nations Monetary and Financial Conference at Bretton Woods, New Hampshire, USA, the IMF and International Bank for Reconstruction and Development (World Bank) were created (Encyclopedia.com, 2020) They were established as a framework for economic cooperation and development with the central theme of creating a stable and prosperous global

Global Business in the Age of Transformation. Mahesh K. Joshi and J.R. Klein, Oxford University Press.
© Mahesh K. Joshi and J.R. Klein 2021. DOI: 10.1093/oso/9780192847232.003.0004

economy. At its creation, the IMF had three declared primary roles. They were, first, to oversee the fixed exchange rate arrangements between countries thereby assisting governments to manage their exchange rates and prioritize economic growth; second, the provision of short-term capital to aid the balance of payments; third, to avoid the spread of international economic crises which included putting the pieces of the international economy back together after the Second World War. While the goals of these organizations remain the same, their work is evolving in response to new economic developments and new challenges. We wonder, along with Michael O'Sullivan, former investment banker and Princeton University economist, if the World Bank, the IMF, and the WTO will come to appear increasingly "defunct" (O'Sullivan, 2019).

The World Bank's loans before 1974 were relatively small which might be attributable to the fiscal conservatism prevalent in those decades. After the Second World War the Marshall Plan provided varied alternative finance sources to Europe that precipitated the move to focus on non-European markets. The World Bank is a component of the World Bank Group, a group of five international organizations that make loans to developing countries. The World Bank comprises two institutions: the International Bank for Reconstruction and Development (IBRD), and the International Development Association (IDA). The Bank's activities focus on developing countries, in the areas of agriculture and rural development, education, health, large industrial construction projects, environmental protection, governance, and infrastructure. It provides loans with preferential rates for member countries and also makes grants to poor countries. Both grants and loans are for specific projects which are often linked to broader policy changes.

The world has changed since 1945 and the World Bank, along with other international monetary institutions, face a critical question. In the evolved architecture of international finance, given the increasingly interconnected nature of private capital flows and the rise of significant emerging economies such as the BRICS, TIMP, and MINT, is the World Bank in its legacy role still relevant? 'The financial markets of today bear virtually no similarity to those of 1944,' writes Jessica Einhorn, former Managing Director of the

World Bank. 'The [World Bank] was created to provide credit to its member countries, and in those days, that credit was often the only kind available to them. Those days are over' (Einhorn, 2006).

In the face of just this one reality, there are some recommendations that the Bank should narrow its focus to countries that lack access to private markets. 'If the World Bank wants to have a significant role on the lending side, it's going to have to be in the poorest of the poor countries or war-torn countries where the private sector has been effectively scared off' (Steil, 2019). This view has yet to be embraced by the Bank.

Regardless of the argument, some 'blinding flashes of the obvious' should define the challenge of the future. The investment funds focused on emerging economies such as the BRICS' New Development Bank, African Development Bank, and the Asian Infrastructure Investment Bank have presented attractive alternatives to the Bretton Woods institutions. Rebecca Liao, a China analyst, writes that the Asian Infrastructure Investment Bank 'was born out of two main grievances about the World Bank' that developing nations shared. First, developing countries have long complained about the conditionality of World Bank loans and have cast their terms as onerous. Second, emerging markets—China in particular— have been frustrated with their relative lack of influence at the World Bank and the IMF (Liao, 2015).

Other thinking identifies the emergence of a multipolar world. This view postulates that commanding influence will eventually be wielded by three regions: America, the European Union, and a China-centric Asia. They will increasingly take quite different approaches to economic policy, liberty, warfare, technology, and society. Mid-sized countries like Russia, Britain, Australia, and Japan will struggle to find their place in the world, while new coalitions of small, advanced states like those of Scandinavia and the Baltics will emerge. In this world of 'competing equals' the World Bank, the IMF, and the WTO will be increasingly irrelevant (O'Sullivan, 2019).

The IMF is an institution charged with a mandate for economic and financial stability, including by championing inclusive growth, and supporting countries in developing such frameworks. After seventy-five years putting out financial fires around the world, it is sometimes referred to as the world's financial firefighter (Scott and Touitou, 2019). The IMF has faced criticism for repeatedly failing to prevent crises and for making things worse for the people it is meant to help. It is not easy to fight the world's fires and the IMF has been blamed for prescribing distasteful solutions. A casual glance at the record paints a dismal picture: three decades of severe financial crisis in Latin America (1980s), Asia and Russia (1990s), globally (2007), and the European sovereign debt crisis (2010s). In each case, the damage lasted for a decade or more and the IMF was blamed for inflicting even more pain with its rigid demands and policy advice that, according to the Fund's harshest critics, too often favoured corporate interests in the rich countries over the poor nations in trouble. But at the same time, extreme poverty has plummeted worldwide—falling by a billion people since 1990 (Scott and Touitou, 2019).

As a significant multilateral organization, the IMF has played an effective role in promoting economic globalization. The IMF has opposed trade protectionism since the China–US trade conflict intensified and warned that the rise of protectionism is harmful to global economic growth. The IMF has facilitated the orderly flow of state-owned capital, while encouraging member states, especially developing countries, to promote capital account openness. The IMF still emphasizes the free flow of capital as long as the extent of the flow does not exceed the financial capacity of a country. The IMF helps crisis-stricken countries recover and return to a growth track.

The IMF has encountered difficulties due to a lack of financial resources. Its lending capacity has decreased, and as the new borrowing arrangements expire by the end of 2022, its financial resources could shrink to half their present size. The delay in reform has weakened the IMF's governance structure. Emerging economies have become more important for global economic development. Yet the IMF's governance structure is not fully adaptive to the new changes to promote global economic development, especially because there is a huge gap between the share of emerging markets in the world economy and their voting rights in global financial institutions such as the IMF.

The Fund has many critics including itself. The organization is open to criticism although somewhat myopic in sharing the discussion of the need to be flexible and adaptable while maintaining stability and relevance. In a market where it is one of only a few targets, the IMF has faced criticism over the conditions it places on loans, its intervention in local financial regulatory control, neoliberal policies, free-market reforms, lack of transparency and involvement, and support of dictatorships.

Though the IMF has publicly identified the need to rebalance there is need for reforms in specific areas for it to remain relevant. The consensus is that the top priority to address is the governance structure particularly the reallocation of quotas (and thus votes) as well as the composition of chairs at the IMF's executive board. There should be voluntarily rebalancing of quotas within the existing total, from overweight countries to the most underweight emerging markets. The composition of the executive board should be adequately representative of current economic and political conditions in the world. The board of governors could revise the structure of the Independent Evaluation Office to make it more independent of the IMF's executive board. Most of the Fund's managing directors have been effective leaders of the institution. But equally effective leaders could come from other countries, including some of the emerging market countries. The IMF's financial involvement in low-income countries has been less than expected. Hence, it should expand its lending facilities with the least developing economies. The IMF should play a more active role in information dissemination. It should provide timely and uncensored information on countries' financial health. The IMF should not expand its surveillance into areas in which it has no real authority such as microeconomic and structural issues (like corporate governance and political governance). IMF staff should be trained in political economy as well as macroeconomics (Bhasin and Gupta, 2018).

The WTO was established in 1995 as a result of the Marrakesh Agreement (United Nations, 1994). This agreement, signed in Marrakesh, Morocco, was precipitated by the General Agreement on Tariffs and Trade (GATT) and other agreements focusing on matters of trade. In addition, it codified an innovative, efficient, and legally obligatory way of dispute resolution. The WTO is the only international organization dealing with trade regulations between participating countries through the provision of a framework for negotiating agreements and resolving disputes.

If the WTO was designed to promote free trade for the whole world, its role is even more relevant today. It has become the trade world's traffic cop by providing order, regulation, and efficiency to the processes of trade. The relevance of WTO is essential for time efficiency and productivity. The use of the traffic cop eliminates the prospect of scores of individual countries each deciding how to trade with each other. Its standardization and regulatory frameworks help achieve systemic benefits that enable greater equality. As economic and geopolitical environments change, these systemic trade routes are more important than ever.

The WTO is the principal forum for setting the rules of international trade. In its two and a half decades, it has helped reduce barriers to trade of both goods and services and created a dispute resolution system that supporters say has reduced the threat of trade wars. However, the institution is under considerable pressure. Negotiations on a comprehensive development agenda have floundered due to disagreements over agricultural subsidies and intellectual property rights, while members have increasingly turned to separate bilateral and regional free trade agreements to advance their trade interests.

Trade rules are being undermined by unilateral tariffs that do not adhere to the established procedures, and if implemented, will aggravate trade pressures that cannot be controlled by the WTO. They are facing an influx of arguments from countries using national security as a reason for tariffs. This uses a loophole in WTO law that permits its members to take any action they consider needed to defend 'essential security interests'.

Members have intentionally immobilized the process by blocking nominees to the WTO's appellate body, a key forum for mediating disputes. For example, in August 2017 the United States blocked a nomination claiming the WTO had overstepped its mandate. The United States maintained its stance, and the appellate body remained paralyzed in 2020 because it did not have the three panellists required to sign off on rulings. Market economy disputes that could be resolved by the WTO's appellate body continue to erode trade foundations. The erosion is evident in the fact that it took two decades for the WTO to complete its first significant trade accord and prospects for new deals among its 164 members are slim. As a result, countries are pushing piecemeal accords centred on sectoral issues like e-commerce or investment. While that may be positive for groups of like-minded countries, it underlines the sense that the WTO's broader negotiating agenda is mired in disagreement (Baschuk, 2018).

Today's rhetoric-filled world with pronouncements of 'America first', 'made in China', 'make in India', and Brexit has fuelled the idea that working multilaterally comes at the expense of any one country's interest. This speaks to the relevancy of the WTO in that its role must not be based on what is best for individual countries but what is best for the global community. In this role, it is faced with challenges that require flexibility to meet the needs of a changing trade world. Individual countries do not always function as disciplined societies when it comes to the economics of trade. The challenge of agreement on some common rules is easier in theory than in reality. The observable national focused rhetoric abounding in today's world is a paradox of agendas. As countries like the United States, India, and China try to put their own interests first the reality of success is dependent on world trade. The United States, with its large consumer demand, no longer has the internal manufacturing or production capacity to meet its needs. China is the manufacturing factory for the whole world yet most of its domestic innovation and growth has been fuelled by its global trade. India with its exploding technological and knowledge-based services ends up exporting much of its talent while it still struggles with domestic challenges.

Framing the Challenges

Population

There remains a relevant role for global regulatory organizations which is simply to keep the basic guidelines in place. This is not global governance but the support of national sustainability that helps countries deal with internal and external challenges. The United Nations' estimates that the world's population will increase exponentially by 2050. And most of this growth will come from the developing world particularly Africa and Asia, which by any definition of GDP and economic measures are currently at low levels of development. Even if there were no other affecting factor, the need for mutual cooperative international institutions will grow dramatically.

Currency

In addition to growth in population, technology is pulling the world towards efficiencies and opportunities. These changes raise significant challenges in an interconnected world. Smart devices, smart cities, smart currencies, 'institutionless' financial transactions, cryptocurrency, and currency exchange stability are complex issues that will continue to challenge global commerce. For example, if a key role of international regulators is to maintain stability, the changes in currencies are emblematic of the complexity. Currencies have typically been tied to countries and have taken a physical form in the shape of coins or bills. As the digital age progresses, the need for currency in physical form continues to diminish. It is commonplace to see money travel electronically from place to place along with consumer use of credit cards or mobile phones to complete transactions. As cryptocurrencies enter the stage there is a further question of ownership. The ownership is not in the hands of countries but private parties. It is entirely possible that trade will become denominated and transacted in these currencies. Ironically, this is a return to the ancient system of bartering which predates currency itself. This basic change of the system will significantly impact the foundation of world trade. If the organizational role of an international mechanism is to impact global stability, this one form of change alone throws up incredible challenges.

Emerging Economies

No matter how they are defined or clustered the reality of the role of emerging markets is undeniable. They will be the main engines of the world's economic growth. The Group of Seven (G7), consisting of Canada, France, Germany, Italy, Japan, the United Kingdom, the United States, and more recently the European Union, represents the largest advanced economies in the world controlling more than 62 per cent of the global net wealth ($280 trillion) (Council on Foreign Relations, 2019). There is speculation that by 2030 to 2050 the E7 (Emerging Seven) representing a group of seven emerging countries (China, India, Brazil, Mexico, Russia, Indonesia, and Turkey) will dominate the world economy. The only large player left in the world will most likely be the United States following China and India in positions one and two. The remainder of the top ten economies might be Japan, Germany, Mexico, Indonesia, Brazil, Russia, and probably the UK. By all accounts, the world order is changing. Any kind of world institutions will, by necessity, have to be representative of the new world order. The make-up of the international mechanisms will have to change—hopefully by a matter of natural evolution. We see some countries becoming more dominant and assertive, based on their increased power. China, for example, has proposed an Asian infrastructure investment bank, primarily through seed funding, primarily contributed by China. Several other countries recognizing the need for trading with China have expressed interest in the concept. Conceivably, the kinds of projects to be funded might be quite different from the kinds traditionally done by the World Bank.

China has announced the investment of $3 trillion in an initiative (the Belt and Road Initiative) to rebuild the physical infrastructure of the ancient trade routes which connected Europe, Central Asia, and China (Chatzky and McBride, 2020). Because this is where development is, the need is, and the infrastructure is, it should be expected that the investment and flow of capital will follow. These kinds of initiatives will continue to increase. They will also cause conflict and tension in the existing organizational structures. The

World Bank and the IMF, for example, have historically seen donors from developed countries. The conflict and challenge will be over what systemic tradeoffs will need to be made. The increase in the number of actors with different interests not only changes the time frame of decision-making but also poses issues of equitable representation. There should be no surprise that we will see alternative institutions being proposed.

One of the major roles, especially for the World Bank, is providing aid donors and they give to some of the world's poorest countries though those contributions are only a small fraction of aid money distributed by developed countries. Recently, private groups like the Bill & Melinda Gates Foundation are playing a larger role in a social market almost wholly owned by the World Bank. When the international institutions we are considering here were formed, private individuals with the kind of resources we see today, did not exist. The Amazons, Gateses, and Buffetts of the world have emerged from the growth of philanthropy. However, the kind of resources and speed of action that these private individuals can muster compared to an institution such as the World Bank pale in comparison. Poor areas will always require capital. As the capabilities and the knowledge of the World Bank have increased over the last several decades, it can expand access to resources that could be tapped into by private investment and philanthropy to help countries' changing needs.

Scope

Ali Baba is a Chinese multinational e-commerce, retail, Internet, AI and technology conglomerate founded in 1999 that provides consumer-to-consumer, business-to-consumer, and business-to-business sales services via web portals, as well as electronic payment services, shopping search engines, and cloud computing services. Ali Baba has surpassed Amazon in single-day sales with a phenomenal $25 billion and growing. Their sales are borderless with expanding agreements with companies around the world. As a regulator of trade, what are the WTO's conundrums in this respect?

It is not a simple question about the country of origin of the goods but where they are being shipped to, and how such trade can be regulated. There is a need for some sort of mechanism in place otherwise we return to the frontier world where everyone takes what they can get and there is no control.

An examination of the impact of the WTO indicates that world trade reached a peak of about $19.4 trillion in 2018 (Statista, 2019). It has dropped somewhat in the last few years primarily driven by a slowdown in China, which was responsible for the primary driver of growth, and a fall in commodity prices. Possibly more important is the fact that some of the 164 member countries in the WTO, that is about 84 per cent of the 195 existing countries, have exploited the loophole of national security to impose tariffs on trade, thus bypassing the rules of the WTO (Baschuk, 2018). Regardless of these developments and the current debate about globalization vs. anti-globalization, its benefits and tradeoffs, there is no doubt that the organization has helped trade run smoothly through the various multilateral trade agreements.

The WTO has acted as an equalizer by granting each member 'most favoured nation' status, which means that members must treat each other the same. They give no preferential trade benefit to any one member without giving it to all. It is truly an equitable society as it relates to trading. WTO members have lower trade barriers with each other. This covers the best range of tariffs, import quotas, and regulations. When barriers are lowered it allows members access to larger markets for their goods. This, in turn, leads to higher sales, more jobs, and greater economic growth. Greater wealth generation has an uplifting effect on societies. This is usually evident in lower crime rates, improved education, and broader healthcare benefits. Probably the biggest impact of stable trade is felt in the almost two-thirds WTO members that are developing countries.

The benefits of free trade have been debated more in developed countries, most notably Europe and the United States, than in the developing countries. Another benefit is the growth in income in developing countries creating a larger consumer market for the developed world. An example is India where the pharmaceuticals industry for a long time was quite closed to outside companies. There were drug controls, with generic drugs being produced in India regardless of recognized patents. When India joined the WTO, part of its membership requirement was to recognize product patents which opened up the whole market for pharmaceuticals companies.

As the shift from the G7[1] to the E7[2] becomes a reality it should not be viewed as a loss of power but as the world adjusting to the new order of economies. This is a point of evolution for the WTO where the old model of relatively straightforward debates about tariffs and quotas may need to evolve. Because there are all kinds of questions about the environment, health, development, and a host of other issues these debates have become more controversial and increasingly political. Many of these perspectives are coming from the emerging countries that require a change in thinking around trade.

The WTO, IMF, and the World Bank continue to operate successfully serving as a source of credit, counsel, and commerce. Through these organizations, we have seen the means to tackle issues larger than any one country can deal with. The world trading system, resilience in times of recession, focus on the alleviation of poverty, and the foundation for the emergence of developing economies is all in some part impacted by these three organizations. To abandon them without thoughtful strategic planning would be paramount to suicide with dangerous and undesirable consequences.

Bibliography

Azevêdo, R. (2020). The WTO's 25 years of achievement and challenges. https://www.wto.org/english/news_e/news20_e/dgra_01jan20_e.htm.

---

[1] The Group of Seven (G7) is an informal bloc of industrialized democracies—Canada, France, Germany, Italy, Japan, the United Kingdom, and the United States—that meets annually to discuss issues such as global economic governance, international security, and energy policy.

[2] Bangladesh, China, Indonesia, India, Nigeria, Pakistan, and Vietnam. The G7 have coined these the Emerging Seven (E7) and they collectively represent 47 per cent of emerging market imports and 48 per cent of the world's population.

Baschuk, B. (2018). Five biggest threats to the World Trade Organization as it faces the worst crisis in its history. *Bloomberg News*, 12 April. https://financialpost.com/news/economy/five-big-threats-to-the-global-trade-cop-trump-deems-unfair.

Bhasin, N. and Gupta, S. (2018). Reforms in International Monetary Fund (IMF): Challenges and the road ahead. *Management and Economics Research Journal*, 4(S1), 19–29.

Chatzky, A. and McBride, J. (2020). China's massive Belt and Road Initiative. *Council on Foreign Relations*, 28 January. https://www.cfr.org/backgrounder/chinas-massive-belt-and-road-initiative.

Council on Foreign Relations (2019). The G7 and the future of multilateralism. *Council on Foreign Relations*, 20 August. https://www.cfr.org/backgrounder/g7-and-future-multilateralism.

Credit Suisse (2018). *Global Wealth Databook*. Zurich: Credit Suisse Research Institute.

Einhorn, J. (2006). Reforming the World Bank. *Foreign Affairs* (January/February).

Encyclopedia.com (2020). Bretton Woods Agreement. Encyclopedia.com, 27 November. https://www.encyclopedia.com/history/encyclopedias-almanacs-transcripts-and-maps/bretton-woods-agreement-0.

Liao, R. (2015). How the AIIB is different. *Foreign Affairs*, 27 July.

O'Sullivan, M. (2019). *The Levelling: What's Next After Globalization?* New York: Public Affairs.

Scott, H. and Touitou, D. (2019). IMF/World Bank: 75 years as the world's financial firefighters. *ABS-CBN News*, 21 July. https://news.abs-cbn.com/business/07/21/19/imfworld-bank-75-years-as-the-worlds-financial-firefighters.

Statista (2019). Trade: Export volume worldwide 1950–2018. *Statista*, 19 September. https://www.statista.com/statistics/264682/worldwide-export-volume-in-the-trade-since-1950/.

Steil, B. (2019). The World Bank Group's role in global development. *Foreign Affairs*, 9 April.

Travel Independent (2016). How many countries are there? *Travel Independent*. http://www.travelindependent.info/countries-howmany.htm#:~:text=In%201950%2C%2089.,the%20new%20countries%20are%20tiny.

United Nations (1994). Marrakesh Agreement. *United Nations Treaties*, 15 April. https://treaties.un.org/doc/publication/unts/volume%201867/volume-1867-i-31874-english.pdf.

WorldOmeter (2020). Countries in the world. *WorldOmeter*. https://www.worldometers.info/geography/how-many-countries-are-there-in-the-world/.

SECTION 2

BARRIERS TO INTERCONNECTIVITY

5
Ideology versus Ideology

We cannot examine human history without recognizing the basic character of the human animal. Humans are not only sentient but also cognizant beings with the ability to apply critical thinking skills, reach conclusions, resolve problems, and embrace ideologies that are not always universal. This characteristic has led us down various paths both beneficial and detrimental. Today's world remains true to its legacy with observable trends in diverse ideas impacting an interconnected world. This chapter examines some of these diversities by looking at the history of nationalism and inter-nationalism, how borders tend to be designed, the rise of the nation-state, the rise in global governance, and multicultural thoughts and attitudes around the world.

Jan Nederveen Pieterse, University of California, in his book *Globalization and Culture* (Pieterse, 2015: 43) states that:

> The awareness of the world 'becoming smaller' and cultural difference receding coincides with a growing sensitivity to cultural difference. The increasing salience of cultural difference forms part of a general cultural turn, which involves a wider self-reflection of modernism. Modernization has been advancing like a steamroller, erasing cultural and biological diversity in its way, and now not only the gains (rationalization, standardization, control) but also the losses (alienation, disenchantment, displacement) are becoming apparent. Stamping out cultural diversity has been a form of disenchantment of the world.

Psychologists and sociologists tell us that when humans are faced with unknown circumstances their first tendencies are fight or flight. Pieterse's characterization of the effect of globalization on cultural diversity is a symbolic framing of the puzzling tension that

Global Business in the Age of Transformation. Mahesh K. Joshi and J.R. Klein, Oxford University Press.

has intensified at the speed of change. These primal fight or flight human tendencies do have an obvious alternative that is become more evident in today's interconnected world. The option of adapting and actively seeking common ground has become part of a basic character set of some developed countries and many more emerging economies. Regardless of the stressful barriers of corruption, governance, resource management, leadership, and other shared traits of emerging countries, there is a fundamental cultural sensitivity which tends to exhibit different value priorities than are observable in developed countries. It may be part of the egalitarian nature of technological diffusion as a driver of globalization that has resulted in a cultural focus on human value as a key to economic success. Though the rhetorical stage may be cornered by one position or another, observation from academics and practitioners alike indicates a discernible bias towards common ground and shared social benefit. Before the discussion gets focused on differences it is prudent to examine the journey taken.

Borders

Even before the existence of official borders communities defined their boundaries usually based on some geographic feature like a valley, river, mountain range, or an ocean. As cultures evolved and grew these communities began taking on other characteristics. The parameters of space based on race, ethnicity, language, or ideology needed more definition than simple geography could supply. Communities evolved into city-states with clear borders sometimes becoming walls with the expansion of the community growing outside the border. They developed systems of governance that typically became ruled by an individual or small group whose ambition resulted in expansion across barriers whether geographical or the border of some other community. History is mostly the story of what happened next.

As nations and nation-states emerged, borders began to be established and changed in different ways. Geographical features are still a factor in defining borders. For example, Australia is an island nation with borders defined by the ocean and India is defined by its mountains and oceans. In some cases, there has been an agreement that was mutually accepted by separate countries to change their borders. Examples are the 1990 reunification of East and West Germany (BBC, 2019), the splitting of India into India and Pakistan at the end of the British colonial rule in 1947 (History, 2020a), and the joining of North and South Vietnam after the 1976 war (History. com, 2020b). This method also includes annexation and secession. Border changes are often not as harmless as mutual agreement but are the result of aggressive behaviour. War has continued to be a major reason for border movement with conquest being evident throughout history.

Conflicts many times lead to another form of border change: treaties. They typically happen at the end of a war and contain terms and border definitions as a result of dictates of the conqueror or acquiescence of the conquered.

A final way of changing borders is through purchase. Probably the most well-known of these is the Louisiana Purchase (History. com, 2019) when the United States acquired a good portion of middle America from the French and the purchase of Alaska from Russia (History.com, 2020c). The existence of borders is not usually a primary issue. Border changes around the globe are common with some national or regional borders constantly in play. The issue is how countries regulate, secure, and open to cross-border travel, commerce or trade, and migration.

History of Nations

Benedict Anderson, the renowned Cornell University political scientist, described nations as an 'imagined community' (Anderson, 2006). This is based on a sense of connection of a group of people that share some quantifiable condition. Whether it is a place, language, ethnicity, ideology, or some other common experience the community, ironically in a kind of mini globalization approach, begin to think of each other as being part of a common identity. In 1882, Ernest Renan in his 'What Is a Nation?' (Renan, 2018), in another perspective says that a nation is not fashioned on the foundation of a dynasty, language, religion, geography, or some other shared value. A nation he says is based on two primary principles: 'One is a rich legacy of memories and the other is the desire to live together and the will to perpetuate the value of the heritage that one has received in an undivided form' (Renan, 2018: 261).

At its essence a nation is defined by the *Oxford English Dictionary* as 'A large body of people united by common descent, history, culture, or language, inhabiting a particular state or territory'. The concept of a united social group finds an abundance of examples in anthropology as ethnic groups, ethnic minorities, tribe, clans, races, etc. They range from relatively simple communities to fairly complex hierarchical, cultural, and political societies. Prehistoric humans used the community for subsistence and security. The world's religious literature is replete with examples of tribes or homogeneous groups each with their own common identity and each with its concept of sovereignty. The nomenclature begins to change as does the cultural sensitivity and the interpretation of the fight or flight syndrome. We see it take the shape of aggressive groups of one kind or another like the Norse tribes, Attila the Hun, dynastic China, the Roman and Byzantine empires, and others that continued to 'bake' 'them and us' into cultures around the world. This significantly strengthened the legacy of large-scale solidarity and identity that is the basic political and cultural norm in today's world.

The Rise of the Nation-State

The origin of the nation-state is a topic of some debate among scholars. The position of some is based on the theory that nation-states did not develop out of political innovation, undiscovered process, or a purely random conglomeration of political and historic events. They point directly to the fifteenth-century intellectual discoveries in political geography, political economy, capitalism, cartography, and advances in technologies (Rigg, 2017). These technological growths and intellectual discoveries were the cause of nation-state development. A second position is that the nation happened first and in them a sentiment for sovereignty resulted in the evolution of the nation-state (Rigg, 2017). A third opinion holds that nationalism is a product of government policies to coalesce and update nations already in existence. Facilitated by advances in mass literacy, media, and education most of these scholars place the primary development of the nation-state in nineteenth-century Europe (Rigg, 2017).

Unlike earlier nations, nation-states have their own individualities. Nation-states' attitude to their territory is almost sacred and most certainly non-transferable. They see changes in population size and national power only because of the changes inside of their rigid borders. Border types also differ with some defined only by the area occupied by the national group while others are space-based on criteria such as rivers or mountain ranges. The biggest difference between nations and nation-states is the extent to which they use their status as an instrument of national unity, societal stability, cultural life, and economic leverage. With centralized and uniform public administration they encouraged economic unity by eliminating internal customs and tolls, creating and maintaining national transportation systems, and facilitating trade and travel.

The creation of a uniform national culture, through state policy, is the most noticeable impact of the nation-state. The term and practicality of the nation-state suggests that the inhabitants institute a nation with a united heritage, language, and shared culture. If these elements are not present the nation-state often creates them by promoting a common language and system of obligatory education with a defined curriculum. At times these policies ignited vicious conflicts and added to ethnic separation but where they worked the uniformity of the population increased and cross-border diversity became more pronounced.

Nationalism

What is nationalism? When did it emerge and what are the identity-oriented implications affecting the world? The idea of nationalism emerged at the end of the eighteenth century and the beginning of the nineteenth (Kohn, 2020). One of the first great events in this development was the American Declaration of Independence in 1776 with its statement; 'When in the course of human events, it becomes necessary for one people to dissolve the political bonds which have connected them with another' (National Archives, 1776). In 1789 the French Revolution produced another powerful statement: 'All sovereignty rests essentially in the nation. Nobody may exercise authority which does not come from the nation expressly' (Yale Law School, 1789). What these first events do is attempt to provide a solution to what Sir Ivor Jennings (Vice-Chancellor of University of Cambridge, educator and expert in constitutional law) once described as 'the great gaping hole in representative government' that is democracy (Madden, 1956).

It seems straightforward to postulate 'let the people decide'. However, people cannot decide until somebody decides who 'the people' are. The nation, and therefore nationalism emerges as a way to answer this question. The people are the nation. What then is the nation? The nation is also a disputed concept and it can be defined in terms of ethnicity, a primal sense of ancient origins, or lost memories (Leerssen, 2018). It can also be defined in terms of civic identity such as lived experience under shared political institutions in common space on the map, creating a common culture (Leerssen, 2018). Between these two different definitions, the people and civic identity, there is a whole range of potentially contradictory implications in terms of politics.

Nationalism seeks to preserve and foster a nation's traditional cultures and cultural revivals have been associated with nationalist movements. It also encourages pride in national achievements and is closely linked to patriotism. Nationalism is often combined with other ideologies such as conservatism, socialism, and populism (Smith, 2010).

A subset of nationalism is populism. Populism is based on the belief that the people should be in power, which by implication they are not, but instead power lies in the hands of an elite that does not fully represent the people. In this mindset, people are defined in ethnic, racial, cultural, linguistic, or social terms, or by political values. Populism is accompanied by verbose and abundant dialogues and conversations. In today's iteration, populism is a political philosophy urging social and political system change that favours 'the people' over 'the elites' or the common people over wealthy people (Palmer, 2019). Today we see much debate over the different forms populism can take.

Issues of nationalism and populism were apparent in the UK's 2016 Brexit referendum and vote to leave the European Union (EU). For example, the majority of people in Scotland voted to remain in the EU, and Scottish nationalists argued that the Brexit vote justified a further referendum on Scottish independence. They believed that the collective identity of the Scottish nation would be best represented as an independent member of the EU. In Scotland, the Brexit vote expressed a clear sense of the nation's positive view of the relationship between Scotland and the EU.

Ireland offers another example of nationalism. Irish nationalism was heightened by the 1922 creation of the Irish Free State as a result of the Anglo-Irish Treaty in 1921, with six counties in the north opting out of the arrangement (Hopkinson, 2004), and Ireland's subsequent establishment as a Republic in 1949. More recently, the UK's withdrawal from the EU has created difficulties for the special relationships between the Irish Republic and the UK especially concerning the issues of the free movement of people and goods between Ireland and the six counties.

The ideals of nationalism tinged with populism were highlighted in the Brexit vote. There was a clear split between those who saw their identity as being grounded in a specific place and those who wished to retain a cosmopolitan identity as part of a wider European community. Many in England, for example, with its shared cultural activities, common language, and sense of history pushed back against recent waves of immigration and the potential different values it brought. In contrast, the Remain voters, representing 48 per cent of the British people, identified with the EU and saw their destiny as remaining part of the wider European community (Spratt, 2018).

The final point in the nationalism discussion is the generational divide. Again Brexit illuminates a foundational issue becoming significantly more evident in the UK and other elections. The generational divide indicates that older voters are more likely to make a conservative choice. They are more likely to feel their identity as place-based and have a longer history of electoral participation. The younger generation, which has historically not engaged in much political debate, generally voted to remain in the EU. The nationalism displayed in the Brexit campaign encouraged the polarization of the electorate between the old and the young (Harris, 2020).

Internationalism

Internationalism is almost a synonym for globalization. Internationalism is a political principle which transcends nationalism and advocates a greater political or economic cooperation among nations and people (Arora, 2011).

Internationalists generally believe that people around the world should unite across national, political, cultural, racial, or class boundaries to advance their common interests. They advocate for governments to cooperate because of their mutual long-term interests and that common interest is of greater importance than short-term disputes (Sluga and Clavin, 2017).

Globalization means connecting the economies of the world for free trade and economic policies to integrate the world into the global village. Globalization is at the core of the policy planning by the International Monetary Fund (IMF) and United Nations. It is the process of opening up national economies within a framework of common rules and regulations. Internationalization involves the production of goods or services that have the capability of entering into international markets according to standards that are globally accepted. Its goal is to expand business and enter into the markets in different countries. It is a process in which businesses, firms or individuals become open to other countries, whether for goods supply, customer base or such other demand fulfilment (Arora, 2011). Both ideologies are on the same track with globalization taking a more structured and 'controlled' approach and internationalism taking a more pragmatic approach.

World Governance

World governance is the concept of a universal political authority with jurisdiction over all people, giving way to a global government and a single state with jurisdiction over the entire world. Such a government could come into existence through violence or through non-violent voluntary international union (Lopez-Claros et al., 2020).

The desire to rule the world has been a part of the human experience throughout recorded history. Alexander the Great led Greece to dominance of the known world, only to become the victim of Rome's quest for world dominance. The Roman Empire, built on bloody battlefields across the land, was swallowed up by the Holy Roman Empire. The emperors or the kings established governments by appointment and established laws by decree. Variations of this idea emerged over time to give the perception that the people had some say in the development of law. Marx, Lenin, and Hitler reflect some of the ideas which competed in the quest for global governance in the twentieth century. The Soviet Union, for example, held elections to choose its leaders, but the system determined the outcome as well as the ultimate sovereignty of the government (Lamb, 2008).

There has never been an executive, legislature, judiciary, military, or constitution with global jurisdiction. The closest arrangement is the United Nations which is limited to an advisory role, with its stated purpose of fostering cooperation between existing national governments rather than exerting authority over them. Other institutions with global ambitions such as the World Bank, IMF, and the World Trade Organization have influence over specific sectors but not control. Though competition for world dominance is based in various ideologies its potential for reality is problematic at best.

Observation tells us that the world may be headed in the other direction as mentioned earlier. Voices like Michael O'Sullivan (O'Sullivan, 2019) see a future that is moving in the other direction where economic blocs incentivized by ideological rhetoric will dominate a major transition in world economics, finance, and power. This view of the fate of globalization faces a major challenge due to technology. Trading blocs or isolationist philosophies while feasible within the economic and financial realms may be less successful when it comes to access to information, travel, jobs, and education. Consumers have come to expect a level of access that they will not easily relinquish. Some of the most successful ventures in the world rely on international markets. The only way this interconnectedness of the world is likely to end is through authoritarian violence or critical tectonic events. The world has become multicultural and a declaration of the death of globalization is premature. It can be argued that the nomenclature may change but not the substance.

Multicultural Thoughts and Attitudes around the World

Globalization is primarily an economic system of integration among geopolitical divisions which also has a social and cultural aspect. It involves the movement of goods and services, capital, technology, data, and people across borders. Multiculturalism refers to situations in which people with different character, customs, cultures, languages, or religions, live alongside each other in the same social space (Song, 2014). Left to themselves, bereft of ideology, most communities/individuals are willing to acknowledge differences and even adopt some of the food, dress, language, and culture of others while maintaining their own cultural identity. Shared common ground is the basis for maintaining cultural identity while valuing the ideas of others as relevant to the community. Who we are together while valuing our differences makes for stability and collective significance.

This is the upside of multiculturalism. The other face of the coin could be summed up as 'identity politics'. This idea uses differences as a tool to either bolster the power position of one identity group or marginalize or ostracize some other identity. Typically, these views are centred on native or subnational groups (Aborigines, Inuit, Maori, Native Americans, etc.) and discriminated groups (race, gender, ethnicity, sexuality, etc.) (Garza, 2019). This approach often fosters separation and polarization, feeding frustration and the types of instability that cause cultural upheaval that can last for generations (Song, 2014).

Ideology vs. Ideology

In this chapter, we have presented examples of only some of the prominent ideologies in today's connected world. We are reminded of this every time we look at the news or listen to the global commentary. Arab vs. Jew, Democrat vs. Republican, Muslim vs. Hindu, white vs. black, Asian vs. Hispanic—there is no shortage of frustration and bloodshed. It has become a generational problem which can only be solved by all of us. The process begins by discovering our common values, what is the same about us and not what is different, and then being aware that everyone has their own story and none of the stories are the same. Each story is true to its teller and that is the first revelation. How can we find what we have in common if we do not listen to other stories?

Then we need to take responsibility and realize that we are not slaves to the basic human fight or flight instinct. Our story may not be the only valid one. This need not mean that we abandon all our treasured ideas but it does require a willingness to hear other people's narrative. Understanding begins with where we feel safe together. The radical concept of kindness and sensitivity creates, in different societal and organizational settings, an innovative mix of personal views, policies, and potentials (Haskins et al., 2018). The thought process may not be evident, but it is essential for the success of our organizations, and the future of our global community.

Bibliography

Anderson, B. (2006). *Imagined Communities: Reflections on the Origin and Spread of Nationalism*. London: Verso.

Arora, N. (2011). *Political Science*. New York: McGraw-Hill.

BBC (2019). Fall of Berlin Wall: How 1989 reshaped the modern world. *BBC*, 5 November. https://www.bbc.com/news/world-europe-50013048.

Garza, A. (2019). Identity politics: Friend or foe? https://belonging.berkeley.edu/identity-politics-friend-or-foe.

Harris, J. (2020). The gap between young and old has turned Britain into a dysfunctional family. *The Guardian*, 12 January.

Haskins, G., Tomas, M., and Johri, L. (eds.) (2018). *Kindness in Leadership*. Abingdon: Routledge.

History.com (2019). Louisiana Purchase. https://www.history.com/topics/westward-expansion/louisiana-purchase.

History.com (2020a). India and Pakistan win independence. https://www.history.com/this-day-in-history/india-and-pakistan-win-independence.

History.com (2020b). Vietnam War timeline. https://www.history.com/topics/vietnam-war/vietnam-war-timeline.

History.com (2020c). Why the purchase of Alaska was far from 'folly'. https://www.history.com/news/why-the-purchase-of-alaska-was-far-from-folly.

Hopkinson, M. (2004). *Green Against Green—The Irish Civil War: A History of the Irish Civil War*. Dublin: Gill & Macmillan.

Kohn, H. (2020). Nationalism. *Encyclopedia Britannica*. https://www.britannica.com/topic/nationalism.

Lamb, H. (2008). *The Rise of Global Governance, and the Agenda 21*. Self-published.

Leerssen, J. (ed.) (2018). *Encyclopedia of Romantic Nationalism in Europe*. Amsterdam: Amsterdam University Press.

Lopez-Claros, A., Dahl, A. L. and Groff, M. (2020). *Global Governance and the Emergence of Global Institutions for the 21st Century*. Cambridge: Cambridge University Press.

Madden, A. F. (1956). Book review of *The Approach to Self Government* by Ivor Jennings. *Parliamentary Affairs*, 10, 121–2.

National Archives (1776). Declaration of Independence: A transcription. https://www.archives.gov/founding-docs/declaration-transcript.

O'Sullivan, M. (2019). *The Levelling: What's Next After Globalization?* New York: Public Affairs.

Palmer, T. G. (2019). CATO Institute. https://www.cato.org/publications/commentary/terrifying-rise-authoritarian-populism.

Pieterse, J. N. (2015). *Globalization and Culture*. Lanham, MD: Rowman & Littlefield.

Renan, E. (2018). *What Is a Nation? and Other Political Writings*, trans. and ed. M. F. N. Giglioli. New York: Columbia University Press.

Rigg, M. (2017). The relevance of borders in the 21st century. Thesis, Maxwell Air Force Base, School of Advanced Air and Space Studies. Alabama.

Sluga, G. and Clavin, P. (eds.) (2017). *Internationalisms: A Twentieth-Century History*. Cambridge: Cambridge University Press.

Smith, A. (2010). *Nationalism: Theory, Ideology, History*. Cambridge: Polity Press.

Song, S. (2014). Multiculturalism. In E. N. Zalta (ed.), *The Stanford Encyclopedia of Philosophy*. https://plato.stanford.edu/entries/multiculturalism/.

Spratt, V. (2018). The truth about young people and Brexit. *BBC*, 5 October. https://www.bbc.co.uk/bbcthree/article/b8d097b0-3ad4-4dd9-aa25-af6374292de0.

Yale Law School (1789). Declaration of the Rights of Man—1789. https://avalon.law.yale.edu/18th_century/rightsof.asp.

6

Old Beneficiaries, New Critics

There is a unique system of thought that has historically been lurking in the undercurrent of global interaction for centuries. It is not an 'ism' that is simple to define. It is a result of a legacy of intersection, dissection, and interaction between groups of people, from those just over the hill to those that live on the other side of the world. That thought process is the ongoing search for common ground, the continual hunt for definition, and the perceived necessity for discriminating differences that have led us through wars, violence, hardships, and glorious celebrations of understanding and achievement. Ideas like nationalism can be a powerful means of achieving goals as a country. It can also be a device of manipulation by groups or leadership that can lead to more dire consequences. Internationalism is the principle of cooperation among nations, for the promotion of their common good, but which can, without thoughtful management, be a vehicle to decimate communities and nations. From democracy to oligarchy, monarchy to republic, authoritarian to libertarian regimes, the legacy of global interconnectivity has its beneficiaries and critics, which through history may be interchangeable. More than anything this chapter investigates the axiom 'the more things change, the more they stay the same'. It presents the commonality of ideologies within the cycle of change and how the role of beneficiary and critic may simply be a matter of timing.

Political discontent has been central to the globalization backlash. Dissatisfaction has taken the form of large increases in voting for extremist political parties, the emergence of new parties and movements, and challenges from within existing parties. Large numbers of voters have rejected existing political institutions, parties, and politicians, often in favour of populists of the right or

Global Business in the Age of Transformation. Mahesh K. Joshi and J.R. Klein, Oxford University Press.
© Mahesh K. Joshi and J.R. Klein 2021. DOI: 10.1093/oso/9780192847232.003.0006

left whose common themes include scepticism about economic integration and resentment of ruling elites. In the United States, both Bernard Sanders and Donald Trump ran on programmes that were openly hostile to international trade, investment, and finance; Trump also campaigned in favour of tighter controls on immigration. In Europe, the populist turn of the right has largely centred on antagonism to European integration, and often to immigration; left populism has mostly attacked austerity programmes associated with the European Union's disastrous attempts to manage the Eurozone debt crisis (Frieden, 2017).

Some observers of the anti-globalization reaction assume that it reflects the economic distress created by the protracted period of recession. The hypothesis was that as economies improve the anti-globalization sentiment would diminish. However, around the world as the recovery from economic downturn has gathered steam and unemployment has dropped the 'anti' sentiment has grown stronger. It appears that public attitudes of cultural liberalization, immigration, national sovereignty, and the lack of response from transnational institutions have precipitated the increase of anti-globalization. If the economic argument was valid then ideological shifts in places like Britain, Italy, Turkey, India, France, and the United States would have been unlikely.

The world has been buzzing with rhetoric and ideologies generally categorized as one kind of 'ism' or another. Whether populism, nationalism, protectionism, cosmopolitanism, or general scepticism, they have all been grounded in the anti-globalization camp. There have been varieties of 'isms' in the past. Russia had its own species during the 1870s and 1880s. A similar, though politically less radical version, grew up in the United States during the 1890s and reappeared in different iterations several times thereafter. Many varieties of populist ideology became a major problem in Latin America during the post-war years. These ideologies migrated towards Europe where they did not have much foothold in the past but are more widespread today. 'Isms' ideologies have also assumed international forms morphing from their original national flavour. The trend of rising support for populist extremist parties has been one of the most striking developments in modern European politics (Taşci, 2019). Events like Brexit, the general rise of anti-establishment ideologies, and the extreme political parties in Western Europe are viewed by some as a threat not only to Europe but worldwide.

The Euro-sceptic triumph in Britain may encourage other governments to try to exit the EU and/or nationalists' attempts to transform the EU from the inside, which promises to frustrate further European integration. Nationalist parties such as Fidesz in Hungary, Law and Justice in Poland, and Lega in Italy—which promote the idea of an alliance of nation-states hostile to Muslims and liberal cosmopolitanism—constitute a front of opposition to European solutions behind which other governments, with reluctant publics, can hide. In such an environment, French President Emmanuel Macron's call for a European Renaissance, with ambitious proposals such as an overhaul of the Schengen Zone,[1] is more political than practical (Belin and Reinert, 2020).

Populism is an idea that has been around for a long time. The new populism began to emerge in Europe and the United States over the last twenty years. It was the economic crisis of 2008 that exposed some underlying systemic weaknesses and problems. It adds to the levels of economic insecurity that affect the entire world. This is a long-term spectacle and is also a trend not just on the conservative right but also on the left. There are a lot of people, whether young people who are more international and cosmopolitan or older people who are more traditionalist, who have great doubts about the direction in which the global world economy has been moving.

Personalist nationalist leadership on the rise in China, India, the United States, Brazil, Russia, Turkey, Saudi Arabia, and elsewhere points to a world that is completely antithetical to the globalization model. It is a world where nations favour narrow interests over 'universal' values, compete or cooperate in zero-sum games, and

---

[1] The Schengen Area is a zone where 26 European countries abolished their internal borders, for the free and unrestricted movement of people, in harmony with common rules for controlling external borders and fighting criminality by strengthening the common judicial system and police cooperation.

where authoritarian regimes threaten liberalism. In this world, the European Union's normative power is less attractive and its voice weaker. When Moscow annexes Crimea, Beijing ignores UN arbitration in the South China Sea, or Washington recognizes the Golan Heights as Israeli territory, international law loses to 'facts on the ground'. Increasing multipolarity has not strengthened multilateralism, but rather strategic competition, much to the detriment of Europe, which has become a battleground for the great powers (Belin and Reinert, 2020).

After nearly two decades of rule in Turkey by the Justice and Development Party (AKP) and its leader Recep Tayyip Erdoğan, the initial promise of reform has given way to authoritarian and dysfunctional politics. The democratic and economic achievements of the AKP's early years helped launch membership negotiations with the EU and made Turkey a model for neighbouring states undergoing reforms. However, this positive picture did not last long: democratic gains eroded, economic growth stalled, EU accession ground to a halt, and relations with most neighbours grew acrimonious (Kirişci and Sloat, 2020).

Across the Atlantic ocean similar behaviour has been visible with popular discontent tapping President Trump. In the election, not just Trump but Bernie Sanders got popular support for rallying against the elites and powerful. The rhetoric aimed against globalism, the press, human rights issues, and the establishment abounded. Brexit was labelled as a 'wonderful thing'. How populism will impact geopolitical equations and global business in the future is generating widespread speculation. Can it halt or even reverse the process of globalization? The COVID-19 pandemic has prompted much reflection on the state of globalization, its drawbacks at a time of worldwide disruption, and the supposed benefits of retreating to the national sphere. In this sense, as in many others, the current crisis has accelerated pre-existing tendencies. The global trade-to-GDP ratio—one of the main indicators of globalization—has followed a downward trend since 2012, and anti-globalist political movements have been gaining in popularity for some time (Solana, 2020).

Examining the Issues

This phenomenon must be examined as two separate issues: globalization, and the crisis of anti-globalization. Globalization has been hugely successful in terms of wealth creation, poverty reduction, and simply generating growth in previously underdeveloped and poor countries such as India, China, and a large part of Asia. Globalization is beneficial. Chinese President Xi Jinping made a speech at the World Economic Forum in Davos, Switzerland. He said 'there is nothing wrong with globalization. It's a good thing and should not be blamed for everything' (Jinping, 2017). This sentiment and the evidence in support of it are apparent worldwide. It has produced vast wealth, trade, foreign direct investment, and a new middle class across the world. Countries that seem to benefit the most are the new emerging economies with China and India being prime examples. Contrary to many narratives, globalization is irreversible and the potential of moving to a de-globalized world with protectionism and national self-sufficiency is hard to imagine. It has simply become too integrated with cultural and economic structures with supply chains that benefit countries around the world.

Attraction of Anti-Globalization

It must also be acknowledged that there are always winners and losers. This is the nature of the world and that is the nature of the international economy today. In parts of the world where the issue of populism has become more tangible the issues and challenges of open markets and open borders must be addressed. China, India, and the other emerging economies have seen the upside and are beneficiaries of globalism. It is in Western economies, those advanced and wealthier countries, which were once thought to be primary beneficiaries of globalization that now are becoming its most vocal critics. The reasons are quite obvious. Because of globalization, they have seen the disappearance of jobs, the economic effects of open borders, the disruptive nature of change, and the issues of technology.

If materials and goods can be produced cheaper in China or Mexico than in America or Europe, where are corporations going to invest? With this simple bit of clarity, millions of jobs have been lost primarily in developed Western countries. There is also the issue of open borders and the free movement of people. Historically immigration is good for economies, in general. Immigration pushes down consumer prices which are driven by wages. In Western economies with union driven wage levels prices have been embedded into the cost of consumer goods as a result of narrowly competitive labour markets. When people from outside a country's borders migrate, selling themselves for lower wage costs, not only do consumer prices fall but also inevitably nationally established workers see their wages stagnate. The availability of inexpensive consumer products produced by economies with diverse labour and wages structures and the resulting impact on the Western workforce has resulted in a real backlash against the long-term consequences of globalization and has led to the re-emergence of populism. Exacerbated by the post-2008 economic crisis this hyperglobalization has also reduced many social benefits in health, education, and lifestyle. This decay has been extremely disruptive. It has disrupted lives, economies, wages, take-home pay, and living standards. Ordinary working-class and middle-class people have seen wages stagnate or decline. The 2008 crisis clearly delivered a shock to the Western economies.

In Britain and the United States, there is a sense of uncertainty about the world. While people see the benefits of globalization they also see the inequities it produces. They see the benefits for corporations and investors but not for ordinary workers. They may be the losers because of cheap labourers immigrating and jobs being exported. This sentiment has been recognized by politicians who have used it to advance their ideological agendas. There is a connection between the dynamics of globalization in the rich Western countries and the rise of anti-globalism and populism in Britain, the United States, and the European Union.

Amidst the wash of nationalist and isolationist rhetoric, the logical question is, 'Will these jobs ever come back?' It is feasible that jobs will come back to Western developed economies but in all honesty, they will not be the same types of jobs. Globalism and its technology driver are transforming not only the nature of work but also the workforce itself. Without deliberate tactical retraining available jobs will be more like flipping hamburgers at Bill's Burgers or stocking shelves at Don's Discount. The impact on work in a labour market without a full-time unionized job is that there are no health provisions or job security. It is this level of economic insecurity and falling standards of living that is the causal effect of the generational divide between the baby boomers, who have done quite well, and the younger generations who find life much more insecure.

Poverty and the Middle Class

One of the positive effects of globalization is its impact on poverty. Since 1978 when China began its economic transformation, 750 million people have been moved out of poverty. 'The share of its population living in absolute poverty has dropped from 97.5 percent in 1978, to just 1.7 percent today, according to the national poverty line, while per capita income has increased 20-fold' (Trankmann, 2019). The scholarly question that frequently follows such statements is what does it mean to be in poverty? There is an acknowledged variation in approaches and motives for defining poverty. Whether it is poverty lines, methodologies, measurements, or metrics, at the end of the discussion it remains the case that globalization is moving people towards better lives. The worldwide changes are reducing the number of poor and are seeing the creation of a new middle class.

This new middle class emerged as a result of access to resources and has awakened an entrepreneurial strength in China, the entrepreneurial spirit in India, and sparked growth in many emerging economies. The opening of a world economy facilitating selling into world markets has, in a sense, facilitated the drafting of international economic standards; when measured against the United States and European Union this has created a dynamic and cash-rich middle class.

Economic Consequences

There are economic consequences of anti-globalization. Governments will be under more pressure to protect and to keep industries at home, to employ more of their people in domestic industries. The former Prime Minister of the UK, Theresa May, is a daughter of a vicar and comes from a very respectable middle-class background in rural England (Britannica, 2020b). During her tenure, she repeatedly called for more jobs for British workers. Former President Trump and almost every other elected official in the United States adopted the mantra of anti-globalization whether they have populist roots or not. The movement will have consequences regardless of economic feasibility. Whether it will run up against the logic of the world economy and the logic of the market remains to be seen. UK Prime Minister Margaret Thatcher's favourite saying was 'You cannot buck the market' (Leitner et al., 2007).

There are also political consequences. What happened in Britain and the United States within the recent past has had a major impact on the rest of the world economy. Britain and the United States together have been the great drivers in globalization in the twenty-first century (Dent, 2020). As these two countries begin to move back within their borders, this will have a knock-on effect for the rest of the world.

Whether Brexit is understood as the cumulative outcome of several factors that are particular to the UK or the product of broader, wider and more European or even more global developments in politics will pose different lessons to consider. Is it a perfect storm of contingent factors or is it a deeper structural issue that we need to look at? The first scenario to address is the tension between sovereignty, democracy, and global economic integration.

Harvard scholar Daniel Rodrik formulated a fundamental political dilemma of the world economy. His thesis is the impossibility of simultaneously achieving democracy, national self-determination, and global economic integration. He says that the market requires a wide range of legal, social, and political institutions in order to impact the market and ensure that it remains socially sustainable. However, different institutions respond to different preferences. A world that is sufficiently responsive to democratic preference will result in institutional divergence and diversity. However, institutional diversity inhibits the integration of global markets because it means transactional costs. Therefore, a world that is sufficiently responsive to national democratic preferences will at the same time fall short in its efforts towards globalization (Rodrik, 2012).

Democracy, National Self-Determination, and Economic Globalization

This discussion postulates that democracy, national self-determination, and economic globalization are not all compatible (Rodrik, 2011). Choosing two together is as harmonious as possible. Many countries are prone to pick nationalism which falls under the category of a non-starter in today's world. However, unregulated global markets are as likely to be inefficient in the same world and just as prone to failures. Therefore, particularly in the late 1990s and early 2000s, many economies move towards a global or supranational democratic structure (United Nations High-Level Advisory Board on Economic and Social Affairs, 2020).

As an example of the complexity of 'choosing only two' is Britain's attempt to solve its problems with Brexit. Both sides of the referendum promised to regain national identity, deepen democracy, and expand globalization which turned out well for at least one side of the argument. If the vote is framed this way it is apparent why it appealed to such a wide range of voters. However, the issue becomes that the solution itself lacks credibility and is simply the latest version of 'you can have your cake and eat it too'. Therefore, it is not a question of Brexit dividing the country so much as revealing existing deep-seated inequality and social polarization. History and particularity have also played a significant role. The UK has had a very particular pragmatic, strategic, and transactional approach to integration. Therefore it mainly looks at national interests rather than Europe's fundamental values. The concept of shared sovereignty was always viewed with suspicion. Britain is with Europe because they are friends and allies but they do not see themselves as part of the integration. The UK chose not to join the original six in the 1950s. Instead, it preferred to commit to a multinational free trade system and prioritized transatlantic relations over Western Europe. Its change of heart in the 1960s was more driven by its interest to avoid economic decline rather than any sudden conversion to the political cause of European integration (RTE, 2020). The UK was always a rather awkward partner and often sought and received special treatment. The British public never really wanted to be part of European integration.

Another example is the blurring of the notion of democracy, which relies on the concept of a government informed by the people. We use this example because of the primary role democracy has had in the evolution of today's economic world. For people to be effective in their role, they must be informed of the issues through a free and unfettered process of access. In a democracy that is the role the press, the 'fourth estate' as it was coined in the French Revolution (Britannica, 2020a). This role is essential to the democratic process. The process of allowing a free press has not always been pretty and is sometimes flawed but the concept and importance of the fourth estate is paramount to the structure. In today's nationalist and populist environment the rhetoric about fake news and attacking mainstream media from various voices around the world has precipitated a troubling phenomenon. Just as in magic, distraction is the key to the illusion. The rhetoric if repeated often enough becomes some people's truth. The prominence of social media and unlimited access to information makes the role of the fourth estate of primary importance. This also puts a tremendous burden on journalism to remain unbiased amid the fray. Neither side of this discussion leaves with clean slates. The unexpected effect of this two-sided struggle is the erosion of trust in democratic institutions and democracy itself.

Bibliography

Belin, C. and Reinert, T. (2020). The eclipse of the European Union's global influence. *The Brookings Institution*, 8 April. https://www.brookings.edu/blog/order-from-chaos/2019/04/08/the-eclipse-of-the-european-unions-global-influence/.

Britannica (2020a). French history, Estates-General. *Britannica*. https://www.britannica.com/topic/Estates-General.

Britannica (2020b). Theresa May. *Britannica*. https://www.britannica.com/biography/Theresa-May.

Dent, C. M. (2020). Brexit, Trump and trade: Back to a late 19th century future? *Competition & Change*, 24, 338–57.

Frieden, J. (2017). The politics of the globalization backlash: Source and implications. https://scholar.harvard.edu/files/jfrieden/files/the_politics_of_the_globalization_backlash.pdf.

Jinping, X. (2017). Jointly shoulder responsibility of our times, promote global growth. Presentation at the World Economic Forum, Davos, Switzerland.

Kirişci, K. and Sloat, A. (2020). The rise and fall of liberal democracy in Turkey: Implications for the West. *The Brookings Institution*, February. https://www.brookings.edu/research/the-rise-and-fall-of-liberal-democracy-in-turkey-implications-for-the-west/.

Leitner, H., Peck, J., and Sheppard, E. S. (eds.) (2007). *Contesting Neoliberalism: Urban Frontiers*. New York: Guilford Press.

Rodrik, D. (2011). *The Globalization Paradox: Democracy and the Future of the World Economy*. New York: W. W. Norton.

Rodrik, D. (2012). Globalization dilemmas and the way out. *The Indian Journal of Industrial Relations*, 47, 393–404.

RTE (2020). Key dates in UK's troubled history with EU. *RTE*, Ireland's national public service media, 31 January. https://www.rte.ie/news/brexit/2020/0131/1112116-uk-eu-history/.

Solana, J. (2020, July 22). A better globalization. *The Brookings Institution*, 22 July. https://www.brookings.edu/blog/order-from-chaos/2020/07/22/a-better-globalization/.

Taşci, D. H. (2019, January). The rise of right-wing populism in Europe: What are the primary reasons for the rise of right-wing populism in Europe? https://www.researchgate.net/publication/338490815_The_Rise_of_Right-Wing_Populism_in_Europe_What_are_the_primary_reasons_for_the_rise_of_right-wing_populism_in_Europe.

Trankmann, B. (2019). What changes after China defeats poverty? *China Daily*, 23 December.

UK in a Changing Europe (2020). Why did the United Kingdom not join the European Union when it started? UK in a Changing Europe, 21 September. https://ukandeu.ac.uk/the-facts/why-did-the-united-kingdom-not-join-the-european-union-when-it-started/.

United Nations High-Level Advisory Board on Economic and Social Affairs (2020). *Recover Better: Economic and Social Challenges and Opportunities.* New York: United Nations.

7

Geopolitical Fractures

Today's world is in the midst of sorting out the difference between its national fervour and its international character. It continues to struggle with its sovereign borders and a workforce that has no borders. Nations scamper to maintain their self-sufficiency while their populations' demand for consumer goods is beyond their capacity to supply. Societies and countries wrestle with basic inequities baked into their culture and political systems that benefit few and alienate many. Geopolitical practitioners grasp for a handle on the tsunami of technology in which they are drowning while their citizens with access to that very wave are increasingly disenchanted with the status quo. Social media's impact is classless and can be both empowering and polarizing. Tucked underneath these symptoms are the pulls and pushes of an age-old contest between separation and integration, federalism and socialism, nationalism and internationalism. This chapter examines the power of ideologies to enthrone and alienate, empower and marginalize. It looks at the importance of words and observes how their rhetorical use can stimulate, propagate, manipulate, and potentially subjugate. The chapter observes and reports on alienation, mistrust, and inequity that are exposing violence and unrest on the world stage. This chapter examines the anti-globalization phenomenon as it presents itself geographically.

Turkey

Turkey is an emerging economy that has a unique culture between the East and the West. Until 1980, Turkish economic and trade policies were characterized by import-substituting industrialization

Global Business in the Age of Transformation. Mahesh K. Joshi and J.R. Klein, Oxford University Press.
© Mahesh K. Joshi and J.R. Klein 2021. DOI: 10.1093/oso/9780192847232.003.0007

under heavy state protection. In January 1980, a comprehensive structural adjustment reform programme was launched and a major component of the reform package consisted of trade liberalization policies (Ridvan and Sevilay, 2016). In 1989, the country opened up its domestic and asset markets to international competition with the declaration of the convertibility of the Turkish Lira in 1989 and the elimination of controls on foreign capital transactions (Aytac, 2016). In 1996, Turkey signed the Custom Union agreement with the European Union and free trade agreements with the European free trade countries, such as those in Central and Eastern Europe, and with Israel (Kirişci, 2020). These policy changes led to significant increases in both imports and exports. For example, the import penetration ratio for manufacturing increased from 15 per cent in 1980 to 30 per cent in 2000 (Taymaz and Yilmaz, 2007). Turkey was showing signs of becoming an active player on the global stage.

Islamism in Turkey, like all forms of Islamism, was shaped to a significant degree by the prototypical Islamism of Egypt's Muslim Brotherhood but it was never as radical as the Brotherhood. Muslim Turks aspired to a roots-and-branch (literally 'radical') transformation of the Egyptian political system; the National Outlook Islamists wanted the freedom to live in an Islamically 'pure' way within the Turkish Republic by establishing what they called a 'Just System' (Adil Düzen) that was never clearly defined. This meant that the majority of Turkey's National Outlook Islamists found it relatively easy to accommodate the AKP's post-Islamist or 'Muslim Democrat' position from 2001 to 2013 (Yilmaz et al., 2017).

Following his 2007 win, Prime Minister Recep Tayyip Erdoğan declared that there would be 'No IMF in Turkey's future'. Since Turkey made its final loan payment to the IMF in May 2008, it has struggled to open its markets, experiencing economic crisis (financial meltdown) attributable to excessive private and household debt, massive dollarization, a failed coup attempt by a faction of the Turkish military (15 July 2016), fast-rising unemployment (over 14 per cent), and fast devaluation of the currency due to repeated speculative attacks and the subsequent cascade of corporate defaults

(Taskinsoy, 2019). As a result of some of the political decisions made after the 2016 coup, Turkey has exhibited signs of isolationism and alienation from global markets.

Europe

Europe's political environment has been rocked in recent years by the emergence of populist parties, many of which sit on the far right of the political spectrum and question the fundamental value of European integration. These parties generally receive relatively low favourability ratings in national surveys, but their supporters stand out on a range of important issues (Devlin and Mordecai, 2019). In this examination of geopolitical fracture, we will look at some issues that have become emblematic of the anti-globalization and/or populist ideology.

European Union

People with positive views of populist parties in Europe tend to have a much less favourable attitude towards the European Union. The starkest difference appears in Germany, where those who support the right-wing Alternative for Germany (AfD) party are 35 per cent less likely to express a favourable view of the EU than people who do not support AfD (Gaston, 2020).

Differences of 20 per cent or more also exist between supporters and non-supporters of right-wing populist parties in Sweden, France, the Czech Republic, the United Kingdom and the Netherlands (Devlin and Mordecai, 2019).

The Czech Republic's populist ANO 2011 party does not fit into a right-wing categorization but follows a similar pattern: 41 per cent of its supporters have a positive view of the EU, compared with 66 per cent of Czechs who do not support the party (Devlin and Mordecai, 2019).

For some European populist parties that have recently tempered their rhetoric and moved towards the centre of the political spectrum, the opposite pattern emerges. Those who support Slovakia's OLaNO party, Hungary's Jobbik, or Italy's Five Star Movement (M5S), for example, are more likely than non-supporters to have a favourable opinion of the EU. Likewise, supporters of the left-wing Greek party Syriza hold more favourable views of the EU than those who do not support the party (Devlin and Mordecai, 2019).

Muslims

Many European populist parties, particularly those on the right, have been critical of migration into the EU from Muslim-majority countries. The Pew Research Center's 2019 Global Attitudes Survey (Pew Research Center, 2019) shows that supporters of these parties often have more negative attitudes towards Muslims in their country.

In Sweden, those with a favourable view of the Sweden Democrats—a party that has opposed increased multiculturalism and especially immigration—are 42 per cent more likely than non-supporters to have an unfavourable opinion of Muslims. A similar gap exists between Germans who support AfD and those who do not (41 points) (Devlin and Mordecai, 2019).

Smaller but still substantial gaps exist between supporters and non-supporters of several right-wing populist parties in the Czech Republic, the Netherlands, France, Italy, Spain, the UK, and Hungary. On the other hand, those who support more left-leaning populist parties in Spain (Podemos), Greece (Syriza), and France (Insoumise) are more favourable towards Muslims than those who do not (Devlin and Mordecai, 2019).

Russia's Putin

Populist party supporters in Europe tend to have more confidence in Russian President Vladimir Putin's dealings in international affairs. The biggest difference between populists and non-populists is in the Czech Republic. Around six-in-ten (61 per cent) of those with a favourable view of the Czech Freedom and Direct Democracy party (SPD) have confidence in Putin on world affairs, compared with just 24 per cent of those with an unfavourable view of the party (Devlin and Mordecai, 2019). SPD leaders have been vocal about their opposition to Western sanctions on Russia after the annexation of Crimea and have aligned themselves with the Czech Republic's pro-Russia president (Devlin and Mordecai, 2019).

Supporters of many right-wing populist parties in Hungary, Germany, Slovakia, the Netherlands, and Sweden are all at least 20 per cent more likely than non-supporters to express confidence in Putin on the world stage (Devlin and Mordecai, 2019). Still, even among those who express a positive view of populist parties, ratings for Putin tend to be low. Take Spain's right-wing Vox party: while supporters of the party are more likely than non-supporters to voice confidence in Putin, two-thirds of Vox supporters nonetheless say they lack confidence in the Russian president (Devlin and Mordecai, 2019).

National Culture's Future

Supporters of populist parties in Europe vary when it comes to their assessments of the future of their country's culture. Backers of the three left-wing populist parties in the Pew Research Center's survey are all more optimistic about the future of their country's culture when compared with non-supporters. But there is less consensus among supporters of right-wing and centre-populist parties (Devlin and Mordecai, 2019).

Generally speaking, parties that hold more seats in national legislatures or are part of governing coalitions tend to have more hopeful supporters. This is especially true among those who favour right-wing parties. For example, supporters of Fidesz, which holds two-thirds of seats in Hungary's parliament and leads a majority government there, are far more confident in the future of their culture than other Hungarians (a 33-point difference). By contrast, supporters of most other right-wing parties included in the survey—which have less control in national legislatures—are less positive on this question than non-supporters are (Devlin and Mordecai, 2019).

British Populism

Countries band together to promote trade, defend human rights, protect the environment, and repel threats. They sign treaties and join international groups, and each time they do, they give up a bit of their sovereignty as independent countries. That happened in a big way with the creation of the European Union, a free-trade zone and global political force forged from the fractious states of Europe. For the people of the UK, it was never an easy fit. In a June 2016 referendum, they shocked the world by voting to leave the bloc they had joined in 1973. The way many Britons saw it, the EU was expensive, out of touch, and a source of uncontrolled immigration (Hutton, 2020).

Since the UK's entrance into the European Economic Community (1957) there have been arguments urging an exit and challenges every step of the way. In 1993 the Maastricht Treaty, which expanded cooperation and created the EU almost cost Prime Minister John Major his government. It was the same Euroscepticism, in 1999, that kept Britain from adopting the Euro as a single currency in the Union. The bloc added eight Eastern European countries in 2004, triggering a wave of immigration that strained public services (European Commission, 2020). In England and Wales, the share of foreign-born residents had swelled to 13.4 per cent of the population by 2011, roughly double the level in 1991 (Hutton, 2020). This migration, mainly driven by the British economy, was growing at double the rate of the EU (Hutton, 2020). In 2015, anti-EU UK Independence Party (UKIP) received 13 per cent of the vote in the general election (Hutton, 2020). In 2016 the EU referendum—the Brexit referendum—resulted in 51.9 per cent of the votes cast supporting Britain's leaving the EU (Hutton, 2020).

Britain's exit from the EU on 31 January 2020, left several unresolved issues to be negotiated during the transition year (European

Commission, 2020). The Brexit vote was about more than immigration: it was part of a much larger trend in parts of the West that values national sovereignty and independence over political and economic integration. Simply put, it was a reaction against a long-running trend towards globalization.

British politicians learned that taking a question as complex as membership in the EU to a public referendum is very risky. The British people have found that unravelling decades of relations with the European Union is far more fraught than anyone imagined. Finally, some Britons have discovered after years of domestic political chaos and the UK's failure to have its way with Brussels (EU's de facto capital) that their country is nowhere near as politically powerful or as influential as they thought (Langfitt, 2020).

American Populism

The spectre of a backlash against globalization is haunting the world. Brexit, the Trump administration, the rising influence of populist and nationalist parties in Europe: despite major differences in form, content, and degree, all share a hostility to aspects of the integration of national economies and politics, and a rejection of existing political institutions, political parties, and politicians. This upsurge of hostility to some of the founding principles of the modern international economic and political order has now affected many advanced industrial countries (Broz et al., 2021).

The populist tradition is nearly as old as the American republic itself. One of the earliest populist political parties in America was the Know Nothings in 1849 (Library of Congress, 2020). Opposed to immigrants and Catholics, the Know Nothings used the beliefs of white Christian supremacy to seize political power over minority populations. William Jennings Bryan in the late 1800s, Huey Long in the early 1900s, George Wallace in the 1960s, the Tea Party in 2009, and Donald Trump's aggressive, isolationist position are emblematic of the populist undercurrent in the American republic (Frank, 2020).

Populist groups and parties have not always agreed about the best ways to tackle their grievances, but most share a common worldview. This common view is the idealized concept of 'the people' as unanimously supporting the same agenda and expectation that all speak with one voice. Therefore, when a government or contrasting voices deviate from the fanciful 'will of the people', it is usually blamed on powerful interests that have corrupted social institutions or the institution of government itself. One of the greatest dangers of the ideology is that it lends itself to alliances that are more radical and deviant. Examples in the United States are Joseph McCarthy's demagoguery over communism in the 1950s and George Wallace's unholy union between populism and racism in the late 1960s (Lee, 2019).

In 2016, Donald Trump rode a unique wave of populist sentiment into the White House. Trump's populism, which included an alchemy of narcissism and megalomania, shocked the political establishment. The billionaire businessman sold himself as the saviour of the 'forgotten American', even though most of his policy proposals embraced traditional conservative thinking (Gillon, 2018). Trump presented himself as a man of the people, regardless of the danger that throughout American history populism has been a double-edged sword: while it has inspired great political reform movements, it has also been manipulated by demagogues to promote fear, divide the nation, and infringe on individual rights (Gillon, 2018).

The popular surge of anti-globalization creates a significant risk to the concept of liberal international order (LIO). LIO is the view that contemporary international relations are organized around several guiding principles, such as open markets, multilateral institutions, liberal democracy, and leadership by the United States and its allies (Herszenhorn, 2018).

Impact of the Fractures

Populist parties and their leaders, most recently President Trump, challenge the core principles and institutions of the LIO. The fact that the backlash is strongest among voters and parties from wealthy democracies means that challenges to the LIO come from 'within'. An understanding of the causes of support for these nationalist, anti-integrationist movements is therefore central to any explanation of the viability of the LIO or of what may come to replace it.

This recoil has been developing for a long time. As technology continued its disruptive march, traditional manufacturing employment in the OECD countries began to decline as early as the 1970s. Also, competition from low-wage emerging economies ravaged many OECD industries through the 1970s and 1980s, with tumultuous effects on labour markets (Meyers and Schipper, 1992).

The anti-globalization effect is not just global or national; it has a significant impact on local communities. Job loss, decreasing wages, decreased property value, corroding local tax base, outward talent migration, and dwindling public services are not anomalies but common local features. The symptoms of this decay are becoming overtly evident in schools, health, affordable housing, economic alienation, and opioid addiction. There are strong geographic patterns to the populist backlash, and political choices are powerfully affected by local socio-economic conditions. The regional component of these trends is heightened by the growing importance of firm-based economic advantages, and local network externalities. This reinforces economic divergence among communities. The most productive firms and their employees benefit from deeper integration, while less productive firms and their workers face globalization with deep insecurity. And the superstar firms tend to concentrate spatially, deriving distinct benefits from being close to other innovative firms (Broz et al., 2021).

The impact of these global fractures is exacerbated by interconnected financial downturns or traumatic events such as that in 2008 or the economic effect of a pandemic such as COVID-19. They present additional long-run pressures that have added to the anxiety at the community level since the 1970s (Rogers, 2020).

The geographic unevenness of the recovery magnified trends in inequality of wealth and income that had been decades in the making. In this environment, it was easier for populist politicians and parties to mobilize voters along anti-globalization, anti-European, or anti-immigration lines. Populism found its principal support in areas where the recovery was slower, and where economic decline had been underway for a long time (Broz et al., 2021).

Relationship of Power

There are two secular trends in the global structure of power that are driving the future. The first one is that we are moving out of a two-century-long period in which the international system was dominated by the West. This vast colonial and informal system has been mainly dominated by four Western countries that have largely run the show for the last two hundred years. That system is coming to an end. Secondly, is the observation that the system is becoming more globalized in a variety of ways but also more de-centric; wealth is diffusing, power is diffusing, and authority is diffusing. These two changes will define the world in which we live over the coming decades. These trends will manifest in several ways in a world without superpowers. Large dominant economies wielding all kinds of power is expected to continue to decline.

The disappearance of the superpowers raises the question of what will happen to the structural polarity theory. This theory presupposes that polarity is based on superpowers that both seek and compete for world hegemony. The basic reason for the demise of superpowers is the inability to concentrate the resources or the authority necessary to be a superpower. Therefore for any one country or even a group of countries to command the level of resources necessary to be a superpower will become problematic. The is a strong likelihood that there will be low or no competition to control the world—mostly because no one has the resources or the will to do so. The United States is losing the will. The Chinese say they do not want to control the world and the Europeans have relegated the thoughts of world control to legacy and nothing more. The Japanese have announced they cannot think about much other than themselves.

Although the world is moving towards no superpowers it will potentially have quite a lot of strong and unique power centres. There is still the will to be a great power. India, through a referendum, effectively has said, 'We want all the stages of being a great power, we want the recognition-crown, but we don't want to give up the status of the recognition of being a developing country either. Basically, our main problem is to develop ourself. Don't give us anything else to do as we don't want to be responsible for the rest of the world. These countries have all tried to run the world and failed. Quite frankly they have run out of energy.'

Besides, there is no legitimacy for the role. The United States has been burning its legitimacy for the last two decades. It appears to be a world in which power is becoming quite diffused with the structures being more regional. There will be much less competition for global power as cultural authority and legitimacy become more diffused. This has major ramifications for the global economy. The world is going to become politically, culturally, and authoritatively a much more decentralized place. The concern is that the great powers will become autistic. They will look at themselves egocentrically and will not be socially adept. US President Trump demonstrated this trait in spades and unfortunately, the potential of most Western powers is moving in the same direction.

In this world, navel-gazing will not be caused by Mr Trump but his example will certainly accelerate the trend. America's superpower status is partly a matter of material power but mainly its social structure, its level of trust, and its role as a reliable ally have helped it play a hedonic role. Trump's administration and his legacy is dismantling all of this rapidly. Now America's values have fading resonance. The message is one of not caring about relationships and consequently destroying the trust of regional relationships. It has abandoned LIO values and therefore sends a confusing message of being a trusted partner while undermining the social heart of America. Likewise in the UK, the Brexit theme is similar in the basic and effective populist inclusion of the Anglosphere.[1] This Anglo-centric idea has been the mainstay of the core for the last two hundred years and has effectively disappeared within the last

---

[1] The Anglosphere is a set of English-speaking nations with similar cultural roots, based upon populations originating from the Home Nations (England, Wales, Scotland, Northern Ireland, and the Republic of Ireland), which today maintain close political and military cooperation.

few years. As with 'superpowerdom', the Anglosphere is now dead in its core.

There is a potential positive side. A more diffused international community is facing an increasingly long list of shared problems. Most major powers have some form of capitalism which creates a strong common interest in maintaining a reasonable amount of the global economy. It becomes the shared fate in a way that it has never been before. There are environmental issues, health issues, Internet issues, and inequity issues that should be shared problems, outside the realm of serious ideological positions.

Globalization's Evolution

Trump's populist assault on globalization has provoked fears of the death, or the slowing, of the economic force that has arguably done more than any other to shape how we live today. Yet those fears ignore what globalization is, and how it is evolving. Globalization is a force both more powerful and ancient than Trump. Too often we think of it—of economic integration and the exchange of ideas, people, and goods that come with it—as a recent phenomenon (Donnan and Leatherby, 2019).

Globalization also is not a stationary event. As the shipping container of the 1950s became associated with global trade and globalization, today a new, far more disruptive element is at work in the world economy. The disruptive nature of technology with new manufacturing techniques like automation, 3D printing, machine learning, and artificial intelligence is changing the model radically. Communication and information sharing have become smooth and seamless and spawned the global nature of consumption and consumer access.

The longer-term structural change in the global economy is the game-changer in this global evolution. Maturing of this change produces other subtle shifts like selling the rights to produce and process to other parts of the world, thereby eliminating the necessity of trade.

Trade measures do not show the real supply chain. The way trade flow is measured does matter. Traditionally, trade data measures shifts in goods by recording products' value when they leave a port.

But the parts of products often come from other countries these days. Even those parts can be made up of parts from elsewhere. That means a more accurate measure of trade and economic relationships involves recording where value is added (Donnan and Leatherby, 2019).

Though companies are often framed as nationally branded, most larger businesses have entered the age of international business. The share of revenue companies derive from countries outside their home market is far greater than it once was. Companies and their shareholders rely more on foreign economies because they are a more meaningful source of revenue and profits.

Entrepreneurialism and innovation are increasingly global. What is bemoaned by many as an infringement of intellectual property may be a sign of a change in systematic patterns. Emerging economies through innovation and entrepreneurs are becoming legitimate global contributors.

Global migration is relatively stable. Though the rhetoric around immigration systems is flourishing, the reality is that more than 90 per cent of people in the world live where they were born. Whether it is for work or family reasons or to flee persecution, we cross borders to live in another country relatively rarely. But that does not mean humans do not like to cross borders. Even as migration figures have remained relatively stable worldwide, short-term international travel for work or fun has soared (Donnan and Leatherby, 2019).

We live in a world that may not exist in its current form much longer.

Bibliography

Aytac, O. (2016). Macroeconomic developments and exchange-rate policy in Turkey, 1980–2001. *Accounting and Finance Research*, 5. https://www. researchgate.net/publication/302921906_Macroeconomic_Developments_ and_Exchange-Rate_Policy_in_Turkey_1980-2001.

Broz, J. L., Frieden, J., and Weymouth, S. (2021). Populism in place: The economic geography of the globalization backlash. *International Organization*, forthcoming.

Devlin, K. and Mordecai, M. (2019). Supporters of European populist parties stand out on key issues, from EU to Putin. *Pew Research Center*, 18 November. https://www.pewresearch.org/fact-tank/2019/11/18/supporters-of-european-populist-parties-stand-out-on-key-issues-from-eu-to-putin/.

Donnan, S. and Leatherby, L. (2019). Globalization isn't dying, it's just evolving. *Bloomberg*, 23 July. https://www.bloomberg.com/graphics/2019-globalization/.

European Commission (2020). European neighbourhood policy and enlargement: From 6 to 27 members. *European Commission*, 31 January. https://ec.europa.eu/neighbourhood-enlargement/policy/from-6-to-27-members_en.

Frank, T. (2020). A brief history of anti-populism. *The American Empire Project*, 13 July. http://americanempireproject.com/blog/a-brief-history-of-anti-populism/.

Gaston, S. (2020). The divided continent: Understanding Europe's social landscape in 2020 and beyond. Brussels: European Policy Centre, 11 February.

Gillon, S. M. (2018). *Separate and Unequal: The Kerner Commission and the Unraveling of American Liberalism*. New York: Basic Books.

Herszenhorn, D. M. (2018). G20 leaders reaffirm rules-based international order'. *Politico*, 1 December.

Hutton, R. (2020). The roots of Brexit. *Bloomberg*, 31 January. https://www.bloomberg.com/quicktake/will-uk-leave-eu.

Kirişci, K. (2020). How the EU and Turkey can promote self-reliance for Syrian refugees through agricultural trade. *The Brookings Institution*, 3 February. https://www.brookings.edu/research/how-the-eu-and-turkey-can-promote-self-reliance-for-syrian-refugees-through-agricultural-trade/.

Langfitt, F. (2020). Brexit day: What to know when the U.K. leaves the EU. *National Public Radio*, 31 January. https://www.npr.org/2020/01/31/801289239/brexit-day-what-to-know-when-the-u-k-leaves-the-eu.

Lee, F. E. (2019). Populism and the American party system: Opportunities and constraints. *Perspectives on Politics*, 18, 370–388.

Library of Congress (2020). Know-Nothings: Topics in chronicling America. *Library of Congress*, 1 December. https://guides.loc.gov/chronicling-america-know-nothings.

Meyers, S. and Schipper, L. (1992). World energy use in the 1970s and 1980s: Exploring the changes. Annual Review of Energy and the Environment, 17, 463–505.

Pew Research Center (2019). *Global Attitudes & Trends*. Washington, DC: Pew Research Center.

Ridvan, K. S. and Sevilay, K. (2016). Opening up the economy of Turkey to the outside world: The stabilization decisions of January 24th 1980, economic situation in pre and post January 24th period. *Chinese Business Review*, 15, 265–81.

Rogers, K. (2020). 1968 flu pandemic. *Britannica*, 25 March. https://www.britannica.com/event/1968-flu-pandemic.

Taskinsoy, J. (2019). A delicate moment in Turkey's economic transition: Can Turkey survive mounting economic problems without the IMF's bailout package? Universiti Malaysia Sarawak (UNIMAS).

Taymaz, E. and Yilmaz, K. (2007). Productivity and trade orientation: Turkish manufacturing industry before and after the customs union. *Journal of International Trade and Diplomacy*, 1, 127–54.

Yilmaz, I., Barton, G., and Barry, J. (2017). The decline and resurgence of Turkish Islamism: The story of Tayyip Erdoğan's AKP. *Journal of Citizenship and Globalisation Studies*, 1, 48–62.

SECTION 3

IMPACT OF TECHNOLOGY ON GLOBAL BUSINESSES

8
Technology as the Driver and Consumer

Discussions of the quantum speed of change in lifestyle, business, and environment are widespread. New technological innovations and business models are threatening existing legacy business players. These businesses were strong and there was little thought that anything could challenge them. However, as with most change those who do not pay attention pay the price. If vigilance is not a common trait and no one is watching where the disruption is coming from, the ramifications are inevitable. In 2001 the largest five companies by market capitalization were General Electric, Microsoft, Exxon, Wal-Mart, and Citigroup (Financial Times, 2006). The only tech company was Microsoft. In 2020 the five largest corporations were Apple, Alphabet Inc., Microsoft, Amazon, and Facebook (Statista, 2020). Most of these companies did not exist when the other five were ruling the world. These were legacy businesses some of which were more than a hundred years old. The disruption of existing business models is not dissipating but is displacing the market leaders of the past. Successful foundational businesses of the industrial era are being replaced. Instagram replaced Kodak, Amazon replaced Border Books, Spotify or Apple replaced Tower records, hotel chains are being replaced by Airbnb, taxies by Uber or Lyft, job résumés and recruiters by LinkedIn and Monster, newspapers and magazines by social media, and retail stores by e-commerce. Many of the new market leaders do not have or own the product but create business models that past market leaders were not able to foresee and changes to which they were not able to adapt.

Research indicates that the reasons for these developments are not complex singularities but are fairly common knowledge and

Global Business in the Age of Transformation. Mahesh K. Joshi and J.R. Klein, Oxford University Press.
© Mahesh K. Joshi and J.R. Klein 2021. DOI: 10.1093/oso/9780192847232.003.0008

not just the purview of the Saïd or Harvard Business Schools. Everyone seems to know that a successful business must be relevant to customers and pay attention to changing customer needs. The theory is incredibly easy but it is the execution that is hard. There are some barriers, gravitational forces that keep thinking stuck in old models. Even five years ago the idea of staying home to shop, getting news from your phone, riding in a stranger's car, or staying in a stranger's home would probably not have been the accepted choices.

So What Happened?

The first barrier to change is related to why it is so hard for some people to get out of bed in the morning or why they keep the same old chair in the living room. People like what they know and do what is comfortable. Given the choice between two products people always choose a product they know versus a product they don't know even though performance of the latter is better. Most companies, even though they know intellectually they need to change, are stuck in the past because it's comfortable. They know what they know and rely on the comfort of risk avoidance. The first important rule is to realize that there is a comfort gravitation that inhibits motivation to change. Therefore the beginning is to understand the mindset of the natural state is yesterday.

The second change blindness is complacency. The approach of many companies is like driving an automobile with a standard or manual transmission. In contrast to the automatic transmission with its simple skill set of step on the accelerator, steer, and break occasionally the manual transmission requires more. This process requires choosing the right gear to match the terrain and evaluating road conditions to know when to downshift or change to a higher gear. The car will not even move without depressing the clutch and engaging the transmission. The process requires constant attention which if neglected can be dangerous. Today most driving is automatic and in cruise control. Many companies today have a cruise control attitude which says everything is good and let's keep on doing what has worked. The autopilot seems to be working. The combination of comfort and cruise control puts most companies in a deep rut when it comes time for a necessary change.

Another change blindness can be related to the difference between playing tennis and playing golf. In tennis, the player must hit the ball and immediately react to what the competition is doing. The opponent's position on the court must be watched. The speed and position of the ball must be evaluated and the return must be targeted to where the opponent is not. The essence of tennis is more than just hitting the ball but is about reacting to what the competition is doing. In golf, tremendous focus is required when hitting the ball but is followed by a marked inattention, walking and chatting with others until it's time to hit again. This is what happens in some business models. A relevant example is Unilever that spent considerable time researching what was happening with their competition. The issue was the singular focus on the competition and assuming they knew what they were doing. The market research resulted in voluminous discussions on matching competitors' assumed strategies. They were golfers relying on hitting the ball infrequently and chatting incessantly. As in golf, the marketplace is not putting up billboards that signal change. Businesses must play tennis and see subtle changes in the market while paying close attention to how consumers or customers are changing and what they are asking for. If they are not laser-focused and only worried about what the competition is doing their relevance is diminished.

Not paying so much attention to trying to beat out the competition and not zooming out to examine what is going on and what customers want is a choice all businesses will need to make. Kodak did not lose to Fuji and Barnes & Noble did not lose to little bookstores but they spent too much time playing against the competition which is a malady shared by more and more companies.

The Golden Handcuffs

Wall Street and market capital also have something to do with change and its barriers as well. When Kodak were still king of the still pictures the company was incredibly profitable and regularly came in number one or number two in the global brand tracking studies. Kodak owned pictures. There is an assumption that they did not see the fact that photography was changing and picture film would no longer be necessary. The obvious assumption is that they did not see the train coming down the track. However, in reality, years before digital photograph started to eclipse film, Kodak knew almost to the month when that change would happen. They had crystal clarity that this change was coming. They knew exactly what was happening. It was not a case of being blindsided or not seeing what was going on in the world or where such competition was coming from. They saw it and were precise at knowing when their business would be eclipsed, disrupted, and changed. So what happened? Enter the concept of the golden handcuffs, a phrase coined by Allen Adamson, the author of *BrandSimple* (Adamson, 2006). The film business was so profitable that anything else they did other than make film and process film was going to dilute earnings. In their minds, if they took $500 million out of the film division and moved it into the digital division to develop digital technology the only thing for sure is that they would not be getting a 70 per cent margin in the digital business (Mui, 2012). Knowing that Wall Street is the drive to deliver earnings per quarter, Kodak realized that if they moved money asymmetrically, that is, out of one powerful division into a start-up division, Wall Street would punish them. They could not make what is referred to as an asymmetrical bet, taking money from the successful business and putting it into a start-up. They needed to reward their shareholders in the film business. Even though Kodak saw what was coming, they could not make the type of shift necessary to seize the opportunity. They were caught in the golden handcuffs.

The DNA

The golden handcuff was only a part of the story with part two being of equal importance. When companies think about making major market and organizational shifts they need to know what the businesses DNA looks like. What does corporate culture look like and what skills, capacities, and people make up the company's competencies? What are the strengths and weaknesses? At Kodak there was a contentious board meeting centring on a debate about going digital or staying a chemical company. The decision was made to move to a digital corporation rather than a chemical company. The chemical division, Eastman Chemical, was sold off and consequently became a successful billion-dollar company in the southeast United States. Kodak's pharmaceuticals division was also sold off. Effectively they were out of the chemical business but in reality, they remained a chemical company at the DNA level. They were culturally, strategically, and operationally a chemical company without the capacities, talent, or individuals to become a digital organization (Mui, 2012).

Pride, Pockets, and Paralysis

At one time Blackberry was king of the hill in cellular technology. Everyone who was a mover and shaker had a Blackberry clip to their belt despite the visible and predominant wave of smart technologies. There was a bit of institutional arrogance at the notion of touch-screen technology being silly or nonsense. Even though iPhones and smartphones were exploding into the market it was the corporate mindset that if you are serious about business you need a hard keyboard. They were simply arrogant. By the time reality revealed itself, the attempt to adapt to the consumer demand for new technologies was too little and too late.

A couple of other things that make shifting difficult are analysis paralysis and empty pockets. Toys 'R' Us had two types of store models. One was the flagship store which was probably most notably seen in Times Square and around major urban commercial markets which was a high-end experiential place to learn about toys, experience toys, and purchase toys. The other was the bigger model in different locations such as malls and strip centres where the toys were piled high to the ceiling and where they were trying to compete on price with Wal-Mart and Amazon. There was an ongoing internal debate over these two business models with one side wanting an expansion of the high-end toy experience and the other arguing the price beating model of the pricing game. The debate spawned voluminous analysis on both sides with the presentation of viable strategies and no clear winner. The winter of debate prevailed for a long time and when the decision was finally made there was little or no money left to execute it. The process had an unexpected result of producing empty pockets. They did not have the money to execute the 'price game' nor could they execute the 'experience game'.

Many companies with choices in front of them are stuck because lots of people back the common DNA. In these cases, people joined companies like Kodak because it was almost like joining a civic club. It was secure. People were attracted to Kodak because they felt they could have a lifetime job. What could ever happen to Kodak? It was hugely successful, year upon year. Many other companies have experienced the phenomena of attracting employees that are risk-averse and when they look at change the cultural DNA is always trying to take the risk out.

Another reason that big companies find it hard to change is that culturally their experience is more apt to fall into the analysis paralysis check. The attempt to identify the perfect strategy or decision or profit model can be paralyzing. The protracted search for the best usually facilitates missing the good. These are agonizing choices that need to be made. Most times, however, decisions err on the side of caution and the chance to change is lost.

Proactive Towards Change

A primary driver of being successful in a changing world is to pay attention to where the world is going. The quest to stay relevant and figuring out what will happen is often not that hard. A review of common culture over the past decades presenting various projections of the 'what if we could' views of the technology space was pretty clear. In movies like *2001: A Space Odyssey* made in 1968, there were iPad type devices and flying spaceplanes that resemble the cutting edge of Virgin Galactic (Kubrick, 1968). There was a good deal of accuracy about the 'what' but the 'when' was wrong. Part of success is to try to get the 'what' and the 'when' working at the same time. Getting out of the bubble is a requirement. No matter how much executives try to feel the pulse of what is going on they often lose perspective. Where the leader of the company sits is often the seat furthest away from the customer. This may be the number one problematic challenge of business. Corporate leaders have to get out of their bubble. Marriott's culture was built on the ideology of its founder. Bill Marriott believed that a leader's feet should never touch the ground and never touch the office rug. He was always out in their hotels and restaurants. His strategy of always watching has influenced the cultural assimilation of leadership ideas and has enabled the company to steadily move ahead (Atta, 2015).

Setting the table for change is a conscious decision and requires recognizing and addressing the very DNA of the business and if it's not right making it right. Brian Goldner was a surprise choice for Hasbro, a Providence-based toy manufacturer. He came from a tiny division in Hollywood. He was in the movie business and the fact that the company chose somebody from the movie business to run a toy company was unbelievably challenging. But leadership knew that a different type of DNA was needed and understood that entertainment was essential to redefine the toy business. Goldner has dramatically renovated the toy model with everything from Transformers to other properties that truly weave entertainment and toys together. Hasbro made an offer for Mattel in 2017. Mattel, a toymaker based in Los Angeles, was never able to get the DNA right. Because Hasbro was able to get the right DNA into their core they were successful in shifting the company.

Another reason that successful organizations can facilitate change is that there is a constant re-examination of the founding principles and purposes of the organization. The fresh look must drive the question, 'Is our purpose still relevant?' Conservation International, and their founding chairman Peter Seligmann, started the 33-year-old organizational effort to protect the natural environment of places that were endangered all over the world

(EcoWatch, 2012). The strategy was to fence off the endangered ecosystem but twenty years later Seligmann realized that fencing off ecosystems was not working. No matter how many were fenced off, the society, culture, and community around it continued to pressure the system. His proposition was for a change of purpose from not only protecting but also helping communities around these protected areas by fostering better interaction and symbiotic relationships with the natural resource (EcoWatch, 2012). The idea was not only putting up fences but also creating a better balance. The debate was contentious with many on the board maintaining the legacy protectionist position rather than providing economic help to area communities. Seligmann was driven by the belief that the purpose, while valid twenty years ago, was no longer relevant or effective. He convinced the board to embrace both the ecology and the economics of environmental management.

Handling Change Opportunities

It is always easy to sit in the back seat and say, that was the time to change and this is what should have been done. Even if the change is identified it is not easy to choose which action will result in success. The challenge of changing in legacy companies, if not in all businesses, is that though driven by leadership, it is the 'massive middle' that must be moved. Companies like Procter & Gamble or General Electric that were paying attention to their DNA and realized the need for agility find it challenging to move the middle of the organization. Like an ocean liner, the massive middle is not able to pivot quickly. Though leadership may recognize the need to embrace new technology and understand how consumer, market, and environmental changes will affect processes and products, moving the 'mass in the middle' is usually challenging and painful. In the new business model, technological companies like Facebook are built to change and to move fast. The strategic posture of 'move fast and break things because getting things done is better than being perfect' is a unique interpretation of the accepted business principle that there are no perfect strategies, there are just a lot of strategies that are good enough. The new model understands that if strategies are off by a week the long-term plan does not have to be abandoned. The changing attitude is vertically integrated into the organization. Everyone knows and accepts the purpose of the company. There is a much freer flow of information and there is less hierarchy. It is not just about collecting the data, everyone collects data. It is more about finding the data's voice and being able to act on it quickly. Companies must build cultures that allow immediate focus on change issues. Facebook's culture allows employees to cloister themselves when faced with a mission-critical project and effective lockout of their schedule until the project is completed. Anything that is not mission-critical is delegated or postponed. The mantra of these new model companies is that if it was not done yesterday today is too late. They have created a culture that is extremely agile whereas most industrial companies still plan to build the plant, build the plant, automate the plant, make the product, and sell the product. Even though there is an understanding that the strategy is important the model is more linear and more difficult to make agile.

Another danger for legacy companies is the blind spot of success in systems and process. Industrial companies like Procter & Gamble or General Electric talk a lot about the processes and systems they have in place and their way of doing things. They have been successful in procedures but the infrastructure itself can become a blind spot hiding the need for change. As previously discussed, just as with consumers some companies find it hard to move away from comfortable things.

Rita Gunter McGrath from Columbia University in her book *The End of Competitive Advantage* (McGrath, 2013) reports on research done on the competitive advantage of legacy companies. These companies were built in an era when it was possible to build a better mousetrap, gain a competitive advantage, and ride that advantage for a long time. In today's world, businesses with competitive advantages that are not in a tech business have a terminal prognosis. The reason for most companies to go to market is to gain a sustainable competitive advantage. According to McGrath, there is no more sustainability or competitive advantage. Bill Marriott said,

'Success is never final' (Atta, 2015). Unfortunately, too many companies take success as final and embrace the strategy that of 'we won yesterday and we will win this morning'. The approach of Blackberry that everyone from the movers and shakers in Washington and Wall Street is using Blackberries so let's just keep on doing what we're doing, is bound for the waste bin. Companies are more apt to survive if they stay relevant and continue to shift. Only the paranoid survive.

The Leader's Role

Not surprisingly the big factor that separates companies who are able to flexibly adapt from those stuck in the mud is leadership. Having a leader that embraces change and is not comfortable with the notion of coming to the office every day executing exactly what was done yesterday and hoping for the best is the essential element. Change leaders realize that change is part of the success and create a culture that at its core has a perceptual vision. They build thinking cultures that see what is happening in the market and zoom out away from the classic marketing myopia of looking at the world too tightly and thinking obtusely. These leaders trust their instincts. In the face of launching a new course with inconclusive data, consumer uncertainty, and employees that have not yet seen the vision, the leader's trust in instinct and their drive to execute must be unfailing. *New York Times* columnist and author Tom Friedman talks about 'average being over' (Friedman, 2012).

Successful leaders understand that hedging mentality limits the ability to execute brilliantly. Brilliant execution can only be accomplished by extraordinary focus. It is better to execute one thing brilliantly rather than three average things. Research reports that these leaders usually make a big bet and not a handful of small bets and are associated with companies that have shifted ahead of the curve. Firms that have slowly and cautiously thought, monitored, and moved may have ended up with the right answer but its execution was significantly too late. For example, the Central Park Conservancy that administrates New York City's Central Park had an issue of basic security and maintenance. Though their strategy was sound there was a perceptive failure in execution. While the problem was widely acknowledged, externally and internally, and a valid plan for the park existed, the right execution had not been identified. Leadership came to a blinding flash of the obvious that what was needed was to make sure everyone who worked in the park did a good job. This simple idea led to a basic perceptual change in thinking about the park. Instead of one large almost overwhelming challenge of continued maintenance and security, the park itself was divided into 45 smaller sections. Forty-five back-yards were each assigned to an employee with the responsibility of keeping it clean and safe (New York City Department of Parks & Recreation, 2020). This obvious solution dramatically changed the character of the park. In time, it built pride in the park, each of the 'backyard' park workers, and unexpectedly the park visitors as well. The basic business principle is that 'no one washes a rental car'. A big part of successful shifting is the need to focus on a few things and adding accountability to the equation. The Conservancy was able to execute this strategy brilliantly.

Focusing on what needs attention and driving to execution is the recipe for successful change. Most people know the theory but what separates winners from losers is the ability and willingness to do it. You don't have to be first, you just have to be the best.

Bibliography

Adamson, A. (2006). *BrandSimple: How the Best Brands Keep it Simple and Succeed*. Basingstoke: Palgrave Macmillan.

Atta, D. V. (2015). *Bill Marriott: Success Is Never Final—His Life and the Decisions That Built a Hotel Empire*. Salt Lake City: Shadow Mountain.

EcoWatch (2012). Conservation International celebrates 25 years of groundbreaking accomplishments. *EcoWatch*, 30 January. https://web.archive.org/web/20121029163420/http://ecowatch.org/2012/conservation-international-celebrates-25-years-of-groundbreaking-accomplishments/.

Financial Times (2006). Financial Times Global 500. *Financial Times*, 28 August. https://www.ft.com/content/19e214d6-f7c7-11da-9481-0000779e2340.

Friedman, T. L. (2012). Average is over. *The New York Times*, 24 January.

Kubrick, S. (Director) (1968). *2001: A Space Odyssey* [film].

McGrath, R. G. (2013). *The End of Competitive Advantage: How to Keep Your Strategy Moving as Fast as Your Business*. Boston: Harvard Business Review Press.

Mui, C. (2012). How Kodak failed. *Forbes*, 18 January.

New York City Department of Parks & Recreation (2020). NYC Parks. *nycgovparks.org*, 2 December. https://www.nycgovparks.org/parks/central-park.

Statista (2020). The 100 largest companies in the world by market capitalization in 2020. *Statista*, 1 December. https://www.statista.com/statistics/263264/top-companies-in-the-world-by-market-capitalization/.

9

Digitize or Disappear

In 2011 the profile of the top five businesses by market capitalization contained one company that was digitally oriented. In less than a decade, the top five largest companies are all digitized businesses. There is little dispute that this is the age of technology and that the world is being reshaped by dissemination and development of devices that touch every part of human existence. Technology is the driver as well as the consumer of digitization with technological innovation feeding the development of breakthroughs in technology. It is moving at an amazing pace with no signs of subsiding. From simple tasks like buying groceries to cutting-edge innovation advances like machine intelligence, artificial intelligence, self-driving cars, cryptocurrencies, and e-services including government interaction with citizens, technology is changing the way we live and we do business. For the most part, consumers are benefiting with price mitigation and increases in customer service. The digital revolution is proving to be one of the most impactful events in human history.

Any examination of business in this environment reveals the speed at which the evolution is happening. The change is no longer linear but exponential. It is not just the IT industry but all aspects and types of businesses being impacted. With it has come the ancillary benefit of bringing customers to the forefront. Any business models should be built on customer service and in today's world, it is paramount for survival.

Global Business in the Age of Transformation. Mahesh K. Joshi and J.R. Klein, Oxford University Press.
© Mahesh K. Joshi and J.R. Klein 2021. DOI: 10.1093/oso/9780192847232.003.0009

Digitization's Impact on Conventional Industries

Digitization is affecting every aspect of every industry. For example, traditionally manufacturing has been slow to adopt digitization and must learn the ramifications of adopting technological processes before it gets too late. Four aspects are key to the adoption of digitization. First and foremost are all aspects of sales, marketing, and dealing with customers. The second aspect is the production or manufacturing process itself. It is the whole process from the supply chain and automation to planning and delivery of the products. The third is creating revenue opportunities by implementing innovative models for serving and procuring new customers. New technologies force businesses to rethink what the model looks like and that evolution cannot only focus on cost-saving; it must also think of how to generate new revenue. Finally, for any of this to work, an organization must be holistic in their acceptance of the digital evolution. The buy-in must be from top to bottom, from the board to the individual employees.

Sales and Marketing

In the area of sales and marketing, because of the nature of the business, manufacturers have been in a transactional relationship with customers. The channels are somewhat different. A manufacturer characteristically deals with retailers and distributors in their distribution channels. There is a value in the existing distribution chain exposed by technology. Customers rarely seek a retail salesperson anymore. In today's market, a customer wanting to buy some product will first go on the web and review it. Whether it's a third party site or the manufacturer's site to see the product or review the specs there is a whole new change that has occurred. The availability of smartphones in everybody's hands places manufacturing firmly in a new age where consumer relations have become the key to how manufacturers need to rethink the market.

Customers are becoming more interested in customized products, which leads industry to rethink the system of configuring products and process. For example, the oil and gas business uses many different types of valves in its process. Before digitization, the purchase of valves involved looking for multiple suppliers and vetting them and choosing two or three that were most qualified. Next, working with a shortlist to seek the best supplier fit meeting the required specifications, delivery time frame, and price. The supplier that can make the best fit will be the winner. With the inclusion of technology, the processing time frame becomes exponentially shorter and therefore more cost-effective.

In addition to reducing the time of procurement digitization also impacts the configuration of product options. It allows customers to view multiple variables in the selection of product, machinery, or equipment enabling diametric changes in the whole aspect of the purchase of complex equipment. Consumers anywhere on the globe can have a standard product right off the shelf with a simple click. It is no longer necessary to call the manufacture for product or parts supply. Additionally, the process provides input on how the product is configured. Today customers find their value by providing parameters and feedback on product quality, design, and availability. For businesses, the process has taken people previously involved in the process out of the equation and made input instantaneous. This primarily affects the role of product management in trying to recycle what should be the product features in most demand.

There is a Chinese manufacturer of smartphones called Xiaomi. Most of their product management is done by their customers. They put down all the features that are most requested. They then let their customers upload and download what features they would like to see in the next release. Based on that input they decide what makes it into the next product release plus adding newly created features in every release. The whole idea of how a product is developed is done in collaboration with the customer, which has not been possible before.

Creating New Revenue Opportunities

One of the aspects of adoption of digitization is the advantages to be discovered within existing systems. There are undiscovered innovation opportunities in performance and revenue enhancement coming online every day. All of these technologies have different roles to play and as industries encounter them some will adopt one, others three or four, and still others will use them all.

Innovation, such as robotics, is something that has been known for a long time. It is continually improving with the advent of machine learning and artificial intelligence (AI). With robotics as with any other digital innovation, there is a danger of miscommunication around their role and ramifications. Robotics is not meant to replace people. There may be factories that will be populated solely with machines but the reality is that the machines are made to enhance the role of people. Though there will likely be fewer numbers of people doing the same things as robots there will be a need for people to enhance machine performance and operational efficiency.

The Internet of Things (IOT)[1] is expanding quickly, enabling increased tracking and understanding of performance, entropy, problems, establishing greater communication between machines, and various other data based on applications enabled by their embedded placement. These sensors are appearing in light bulbs, doorbells, thermostats, hairbrushes, refrigerators, and a whole lot more. An example is a consumer refrigerator that is Internet-connected with sensors and a camera that senses when foods are going bad. It is also possible to access a view of the contents of the refrigerator while at the grocery store. This type of technology has application in many genres including inside production and manufacturing processes. If managers can understand when equipment is likely to fail and apply preventive action before it happens that removes a great deal of inefficiency from the system. Robotics are good at repetitive tasking but when connected to the sensors and communicative capacity of IOT are enhanced by connection to a supply source ensuring that the needed repair parts are on hand when failures occur. The entire production operation becomes

---

[1] The Internet of Things (IOT) is a system of interrelated computing devices, mechanical and digital machines, objects, animals, or people that are provided with unique identifiers and the ability to transfer data over a network without requiring human-to-human or human-to-computer interaction.

seamless. Add to that benefit that all of those functions are built directly into the machine with no need for human intervention the auxiliary benefit becomes the saving of time.

A new age is upon us where the strategy is no longer building large quantities of something and simply continuing to build the same product for storage in inventory and inactive capital. Today's consumer is looking for personalization. The new age is about mass customization where people want a customized product that is different from their neighbour's, or son's, or daughter's, or wife's. In the new age, the need to build large quantities will be unnecessary. There will be a demand for customization in manufacture and production. Robotics and the IOT will play a role but another technology that has a big part to play is 3D printing. With 3D printing's capacity of building low-cost components in small quantities the necessity to produce hundreds of thousands of parts to store in inventory disappears. Also as prices fall and quality increases, having 3D printing capacity installed on-site exponentially expands performance and cost control.

There is also the phenomenon of interrelated applications that begins to follow innovation. Not too long ago Google came up with a concept of Google Glasses. It was an odd sight to see people wearing glasses that presented a technological interface with their environment. Many questioned the advantage of the technology and were prone to brush it off as a digital toy. Today this augmented reality 'toy' has become the centrepiece of several applications. It has enabled great productivity in manufacturing and customer support. Augmented reality glasses are being used to train people in various machinery and maintenance tasking as well as enhancement of operational safety. This development has tremendous potential in education, medicine, training, and a host of other applications. In this environment, new-age technology continues to find ways into various industries helping them to solve problems.

The ability to customize production and increase consumer connection through local application of technological resources will increase the speed to market for any kind of product. This ability to move the process to local or remote locations implies that almost all work is being done over some kind of a cloud or remote data storage shared space. Companies like GE, Amazon, Microsoft, and others open their cloud systems to everyone including the development community enabling the development of new applications and services. The sharing of space will reduce the need and cost of local space, enhance collaboration, and create uniformity in the supply and distribution chains. This creates an obvious additional revenue source.

Increasing Revenue

Microsoft is a big digital company. They derive a good deal of their revenue from their existing customers because they have built a relationship with those customers (Microsoft, 2019). They know what their customers are looking for and the sales of their products have surpassed service as the dominant product. Looking at this model and applying it to other industries is telling. Manufacturers of refrigerators or washer dryers or most other products do not know who owns the purchased products. Customer interaction is rare and usually the result of a problem. Enter digitization where there is a sensor built into the product helping figure out not only how the equipment is working but also what is happening inside the refrigerator. It allows manufacturers and customers alike to perceive patterns enabling the understanding of performance, potential problems, and the ability to connect with customers before problems develop saving downtime and building customer loyalty. At the time for a replacement cycle, the customer is happy and predisposed to repurchase. Even if the product fails earlier than expected customer loyalty predisposes a sale to the customer even at a discounted price. Distribution is no longer of primary importance. What is important is the relationship that is established with the customer. Keep the customer loyal and they will return, thereby reducing selling costs that are paid for distribution, advertising, and all kinds of things that are done to meet customers' needs. Every customer is a new customer. If those costs are cut out of the system it is a direct bottom-line improvement. Like all relationships, customers respond best to the interaction that knowledge, transparency, and responsiveness provide. Digitization has not changed that but it has changed the importance businesses put on the frontend of the relationship and the importance of making customers feel important.

Most manufacturers give some warranty and offer some extra warranty for a certain price point but do not have much data value to add which supports the added cost. Airbus is an example of how that is changing. The Airbus A350 has around 6,000 sensors generating 2.5 terabytes of data per day and the A380 will have over 10,000 sensors (Marr, 2015). They use this data to predict almost every possible failure that might occur on the plane. They can also use that information to offer service to customers. Also, think of the head start they have when they are ready to build a new product. All that data is extremely useful in design decisions. They know what works well, what does not work well, what fails often, and what never fails. That data is now available at their fingertips. With that amount of data, they use it to modify the design process and the manufacturing process, and build a much better-quality product at a lower cost because they have the information and have control. Digitization offers the opportunity of enhancing revenue. Even though it is not direct revenue, over time it can become a huge revenue advantage because of customer retention, customer acquisition, and being able to facilitate greater customer satisfaction.

Another example is the Nest product. Nest is a residential thermostat that learns customer behaviour and makes adjustments to schedule and temperature. Based on that success they also developed smoke detectors and other products (Google Store, 2020). Because they already knew their customer base they had a ready-made base to sell new products. The satisfaction of a certain section of customers resulted in consumers loving the Nest product. Because the manufacturer had built relationships with them it became much easier to sell a new product to the same base. This results in huge cost savings and a great revenue opportunity that businesses tend to underestimate.

Organizational Challenges of Digitizing

All the digital opportunities in the world are worth nothing if not adopted by the business. With the amount of evidence presented and observable outcomes of integrating technology into operation, why are organizations still challenged to implement digitization?

Leadership drives adoption of digitization. With this statement in mind what has been proven not to be the road to technology? How does it never get done? Many companies that need to be more digital make their digital intent proclamation and immediately the CEO brings in a chief digital officer or some other title. Commonly the position is not given enough power or authority resulting in the inability to influence corporate culture or make changes. This leads directly to frustration or worse the hire of a bunch of consulting companies to come in and implement things that only get implemented over the resistance of the culture.

The adoption of technology must start at the top. Not just the CEO but also the board. If the board has no one who understands digital technologies and what innovative changes they will bring to the business any initiative will have problems. The first and minimum requirement is at least one board member who understands the transitions and who can be the sounding board on the implementation.

Next along with the board and CEO, commitment must start at the bottom at the same time. Pushing the initiative from the top to a workforce of varying skill levels dooms the initiative to fail. It is wise to build a critical map from top and bottom and not treat it as a knee jerk reaction. This is a strategic inclusive transitional plan over an appropriate timeline, maybe two or three years. The length of time depends on the organization. It should be a phased implementation with a starting point and progressive events built on defined goals such as customer inclusion, capacity and skill goals, or evolution of production and manufacturing processes. The strategy should be inclusive, flexible, transparent, and timely.

A 2015 McKinsey survey (McKinsey, 2015) told us that no more than 17 per cent of companies said their boards were sponsoring digital initiatives, and in earlier McKinsey research (McKinsey,

2013), just 16 per cent said they fully understood how the industry dynamics of their companies were changing. There are nearly 80 per cent of companies that lack even basic digital representation. Though somewhat alarming this is not surprising. Many people on boards have seen success without the digital transformation and it is difficult to change minds. Digital transformation has and is happening very fast. The position that technology is probably for the digital companies or digital businesses but not for this company may result in finding themselves on a leaky lifeboat.

The importance of the integration of technology is difficult to comprehend for anyone who has not seen the transition. Like never before there is such power in the hands of consumers. The smartphone with its easy access to the world puts information at their fingertips. The consumer in India today knows as much as a consumer located in the United States. Products cannot be pushed into the market as IBM did in the 1960s. That model is no longer possible because consumers in developing countries have the same information that consumers in developed countries have. That balance in equilibrium is about the power that the consumer has. At the beginning of the digitization revolution, it took Kodak twelve years to die. In 2000 they had 100 billion picture prints ordered (Disruptive Innovation, 2016) and almost 80 billion pictures taken (Mathies, 2017). In 2012 because of the appearance of digital cameras they no longer exist. In today's world, the same thing would happen in less than two years.

The Future

Notwithstanding the parallels of 'drowning' in the tide of technology, what will the future look like? The future for manufacturing and production in the United States and other parts of the globe has never been brighter. This is the age of personalization as opposed to mass production. This is where the United States and other technology adopters can shine by building interesting technology and service applications to meet the needs of customers and investors.

Bibliography

Disruptive Innovation (2016). Quotes from Kodak's annual report 2000. *Disruptive Innovation*, 23 April. http://disruptiveinnovation.se/?p=148.

Google Store (2020). Welcome to Google Nest. *Google Store*, 2 December. https://store.google.com/us/category/connected_home?hl=en-US.

Marr, B. (2015). That's data science: Airbus puts 10,000 sensors in every single wing! *Data Science Central*, 9 April. https://www.datasciencecentral.com/profiles/blogs/that-s-data-science-airbus-puts-10-000-sensors-in-every-single.

Mathies, D. (2017). This isn't the end of printed photos, it's the golden age. *Digitaltrends*, 16 October. https://www.digitaltrends.com/photography/importance-of-printing-photos-in-digital-age/.

McKinsey (2013). *Improving Board Governance: McKinsey Global Survey.* McKinsey.

McKinsey (2015). *Cracking the Digital Code: McKinsey Global Survey Results.* McKinsey.

Microsoft (2019). *Annual Report 2019. Microsoft*, 16 October. https://www.microsoft.com/investor/reports/ar19/index.html.

10
Smart Selling on the E Platform

The Amazing World of Amazon

No matter what part of the globe we are in technology is part of daily life. Whether invited or tolerated, digital presence continues to emerge and propagate in every area of life. Ignored, criticized, or embraced, the fact that technology is taking over the world must be acknowledged. From agriculture to aviation, electronics to energy, medicine to military, or communication to commerce even a casual examination reveals the explosive impact of innovations in technologies that have two common traits. They are disruptive and they nurture transformation that is changing everything.

In business, the phenomenon is no different and strangely has driven us back to some basic business axioms that have been dimmed over the years. Strategies like customer-focused, price consciousness, and smart brand management have been dramatically enhanced by the e-commerce rocket. Communication, shopping, payments, auctions, banking, ticketing, business to business, business to customers, customers to customers have taken on a whole new perspective in light of the technological tsunami.

In this new age, e-commerce is leading the business growth. Companies like Taobao, eBay, Tmall, Alibaba, and Amazon have become household names. These e-commerce platforms are changing the buying behaviours of consumers in innovative ways. Used wisely they can help other businesses and entrepreneurs leverage their own business. To gain some insight into how this can be done Amazon will serve as the example. Amazon is the largest e-commerce site in the world (AXIOMQ, 2020). It has bigger annual sales than the gross domestic product (GDP) of 153 countries (Macrotrends, 2020b).

Global Business in the Age of Transformation. Mahesh K. Joshi and J.R. Klein, Oxford University Press.
© Mahesh K. Joshi and J.R. Klein 2021. DOI: 10.1093/oso/9780192847232.003.0010

If Amazon was a country it would be forty-forth in the world ranked by GDP (Statistics TIMES, 2020). Its market capitalization is nearly $1.6 trillion (Macrotrends, 2020a). The importance of these big numbers is that Amazon is open and available for business to take advantage of the platform to stabilize and grow their own companies.

Selling on Amazon, Yes or No?

The decision regarding whether a business or a brand is sold on the Amazon marketplace is not always solely within the brand's control. It is a better assumption to say that any popular brand's products will eventually show up for sale on Amazon. Whether the brand wants those products on the distribution channel or not the nature of the marketplace will prevail. Amazon's model allows sellers easy access to create profiles and list products that facilitate access at both ends of the sales chain. Customers want to be able to find products that they want to buy. If they cannot find those products in one place they will look in a different place or for a different product. Today's customers can go online to check Google or Amazon to compare price and availability. If the product is not available on Amazon they will be purchasing the competitor's product on the same platform. No matter how great the brand is or how great the product is or how many customers they have, when customers repeatedly find products out of stock they will simply move to the competitor. The onus is on the brand owner to find a way to create product availability in the channels where large numbers of customers go searching for that brand. Fifty-eight per cent of all product searches in today's world begin on Amazon (EMarketer, 2020). It is challenging Google in the PPC (price per click) customer (Herrera, 2019). It is the channel with the greatest visibility to customers worldwide. Brands that choose to ignore this channel are letting competitors or their resellers take advantage of the vast traffic that comes to it. The blinding flash of the obvious for brands is that they should sell their products on Amazon and leverage the vast traffic coming to that channel.

The second question, beyond whether to sell on Amazon, is more complex. James Thomson and Joseph Hansen in their book, *The Amazon Marketplace Dilemma* (Thomson and Hansen, 2016), identify it as the marketplace dilemma. The dilemma and choice are whether to sell product 'to' Amazon or sell the product 'on' Amazon as a third-party seller. It is not a choice of whether or not products should be sold on the channel because products are probably going to be sold there whether initiated by the brand or not. The question is whether the business should sell product directly to Amazon in a wholesale relationship or sell products themselves directly on the channel. The paths, brand, and distribution strategy choices employed will present different issues, challenges, and priorities.

From a customer's point of view, Amazon appears to be quite straightforward in that it is simply a place to buy stuff. Within Amazon, however, there are two different entities. There is an internal business line called 'Amazon 1P' and a retail business line (Feedvisor, 2020). In Amazon 1P businesses can sell products directly to Amazon and function through a vendor central platform. This means selling on a wholesale basis directly to Amazon with the product being priced, sold, shipped, and controlled by Amazon. The second brand choice is to sell a product using Amazon as a fulfilment centre. A company sells a product on the Amazon platform utilizing a seller central platform inside the Amazon marketplace. The product is not sold wholesale to Amazon but Amazon is paid a commission for the product to sell on the platform. The company still handles all aspects of the distribution channel, i.e. pricing, sales, shipping, and control. There is also another differentiator. Some companies sell a product which is delivered or fulfilled by Amazon. This means that a company is shipping products to Amazon's fulfilment centres and the same sort of logistical operations used by Amazon 1P are employed. The customer gets the same sort of experience as a customer buying product directly from Amazon 1P.

There is a host of differences between the Amazon models that businesses must consider. There is of course a margin risk between a wholesale and retail position. There is also the consideration of a brand's ability to control the content presented on the product listing and the ability to control price as a third-party seller versus going directly to Amazon as a manufacturer on a wholesale basis. The company selling to Amazon at wholesale loses control of product pricing. When competitive pricing goes down on Amazon, or other significant online or offline channels, it is Amazon that will control competitive price movement which can have severe negative effects for the wholesale business. For example, if the company has pricing agreements in place with other retailers they might be required to stay at the mapped price. This is irrelevant to Amazon because their goal is offering the lowest price even if it means losing money. A third-party seller has a lot more control over the product listing content and product detail. There is more control over the pricing because the third-party company manages the price irrespective of competition.

Managing Content on Amazon

Sellers of the same types of product (same UPC or skew code) usually end up sharing virtually the same product listing information that includes things like titles, product descriptions, bullet points, even most of the product images. If poor content was used to create a product listing initially, all sellers of that skew end up with the same poor content unless a seller files a support ticket to Amazon to get content upgraded. Conversely, if high-quality content is used to create the listing initially, all subsequent sellers will benefit. Sixty per cent of customers want to see content directly from brands (Feedvisor, 2020). The implication to the brand is that it is critical to make sure product listings on Amazon are properly created and optimized in the first place. This is also true when it is done by a trusted and motivated reseller who understands the need for high-quality listings. Some brands even set up third-party accounts only to create clean listings for all their catalogue. If competitive brands have figured out how to get high-quality listings on Amazon, they maintain a competitive advantage over other listings because they are more searchable or discoverable by Amazon customers. This means there is a greater likelihood to interact with customers once product detail content is viewed.

Even though the brand may not choose to sell on Amazon, 58 per cent of customers begin their product search on their platform (EMarketer, 2020). That means the brand products are being displayed to a host of different customers on Amazon and a company not on the platform must be able to display products that match the feel, the persona, and the quality of those brands. Whether or not a business chooses to sell products to Amazon or on the site they must adopt brand strategies that match or exceed what those customers find on Amazon.

Once a product listing has been created someone must watch the 'hen house'. There are other sellers that play a more deceptive game. They create duplicate listings that may not fairly or adequately represent the original product and become covert competitors. Brands that invest in clean listings and do not follow up on new sellers creating duplicate listings are wasting time and money. These 'fake' sellers use fraudulent or new UPCs enabling them to direct world traffic to these new sites where only they are selling. The bottom line is that managing brand content on Amazon requires both an initial investment and an ongoing process commitment.

In addition to the two distribution options, third-party retailing and Amazon 1P, there are other options to consider. Businesses can sell through some distributors or other resource on the platform or sell through exclusive third-party resellers. Similarly, there is a blended approach with several brands selling directly to Amazon and also having a third-party account. This many times depends on what product mixes are more profitable through wholesale direct or the third-party route. The last option is not one that is recommended. That is to do nothing.

The Dilemma

There is no question that having the opportunity to access the scale of the market available on Amazon is quite exciting to most sellers yet many times those brands do not understand the consequences of working directly with Amazon. Some brands will lose significant margin and control in a direct wholesale relationship with Amazon.

They also have a tradeoff in other areas of operation. Amazon determines how much inventory to stock and offers certain promotional opportunities that may or may not benefit the brand. Amazon also controls pricing. The benefit is that Amazon has a market appeal and acts as the product's vendor handling sales, shipping, customer relations, exchanges, etc. It owns the products and distributes through its distribution system. Whereas, when a business sells the product in the marketplace they typically gain margin, control, listing, content, and pricing. If they sent to the Amazon fulfilment centres they do control the volume of product. The risk is if a business is putting the product into the distribution channel on essentially a consignment basis and customers do not purchase it the business does not get any income. In a wholesale direct relationship, Amazon carries the ball of promoting, sales, and fulfilment and the business gets the upfront income.

There can be other unforeseen difficulties. Amazon is an open marketplace for practically anyone with a product to sell. The marketplace enables anyone with access to a business product to sell it. The marketplace does not control the product being sold. A product being sold on Amazon without owner permission or desire is a symptom of the open nature of the market where products are being made available. These grey market resellers are interested if a product meets two conditions. First there must be a meaningful margin of opportunity. They must make a profit. There also need to be limited roadblocks to selling the product quickly. Grey market sellers are looking for quick return opportunities. If the margin simply is not there, the grey market sellers will move on to another brand. If there are too many threats to grey market sellers to be able to move products quickly they move to another brand.

There are a number of things a brand can do to make their product less attractive to the grey market. One is offering different prices to different channels. If a price disparity is created across channels with an opportunity for recall and retail arbitrage (buy low sell high) it creates a margin opportunity that is less appealing to the grey market. With certain types of resellers, businesses can enter into specific agreements to make sure that they do not sell on channels like Amazon. Products could be offered at higher pricing creating a smaller margin and fewer opportunities for attraction to sell the product on Amazon. Businesses can create reseller policies that clearly outline the rules and consequences of not following policy. These are unilateral policies and not contracts, which bring the risk of anti-trust issues. Brands can offer manufacturer warranties on products and make the warranties available only to products purchased from authorized resellers. Post-sale customer service for customers that purchased from authorized resellers is another workable tool.

A brand gate or restriction is another option. On Amazon, it is possible but more difficult to implement. It is typically only going to apply to products that have some health or safety concerns. A gate simply restricts product sales only to the original seller on Amazon. Some sellers find it useful to put serial numbers or batch numbers on products. The numbers are tied to specific distributors and retailers. This helps to identify unauthorized sellers' products and makes it easier to track and close up leaky distribution channels.

Another tool is to control the returns process closely. This is not just customer returns but distributor returns and also lots that fail initial production testing. It is important to know who is testing products and what happens to products that are deemed unfit for the market. It is also vital to keep track of how many units are returned and where each unit ends up. Too many brands overlook what happens with returns and allow thousands of new or reconditioned units to get moved into the arms of the grey market. To mitigate risk, companies should incorporate as many of these safeguards as possible to tighten control on distribution.

Amazon Opportunity Land

There are many opportunities for brands to make a big splash in the Amazon marketplace by putting together a good approach to the distribution channel and comprehensively utilizing the platform to dramatically increase visibility. Amazon is a three-legged stool with advertising, distribution control, and product catalogue capability (Biondo, 2014). Brands must first clean up the distribution channel by incorporating the right policies and product protections and utilizing the right legal infrastructure to police the channel. Without this, any efforts spent on advertising will drive sales growth and opportunity to unauthorized resellers to offer products on Amazon. Second, the brand needs to invest sufficient time and infrastructure in creating and maintaining an optimized catalogue on the channel. Otherwise, advertising drives lots of visits to the product pages which with poor quality do not result in a sales transaction. Once channel control and a solid product catalogue are firm then the brand can effectively create an advertising strategy.

Where To?

Twenty years ago Amazon started selling books and began branching into other channels like electronics such as their own e-reader, Kindle. They moved into sports, outdoors, fashion, and grocery. Their operating systems have been honed to a sharp edge. There are a couple of things that indicate they are not yet slowing down. Amazon have a great ability to present their story to the investor world. Despite the lack of profits, they have delivered a vision of planned growth until a point of perpetual motion making them unstoppable. Investors have bought into the vision. Amazon have had almost unlimited access to capital and received some of the cheapest capital in the modern world. This has allowed them to build an infrastructure which surpasses almost any company and gives them the leverage to deliver all different types of goods to customers. They have become the competitive giant that other companies aspire to. Even though some products are not applicable for sale on Amazon such as large equipment and machinery, however, a quick view of their history makes the question not 'if' but 'when'.

Bibliography

AXIOMQ (2020). 8 largest ecommerce companies in the world and no, Alibaba is not the largest Chinese ecommerce. *AXIOMQ*, 25 March. https://axiomq.com/blog/8-largest-e-commerce-companies-in-the-world/.

Biondo, K. (2014). The new retail: Three legs to stand on. *Echo Ship*, 8 August. https://www.inboundlogistics.com/cms/article/the-new-retail-three-legs-to-stand-on/.

EMarketer (2020). Do most searches really start on Amazon? *EMarketer— Insider Intelligence*, 7 January. https://www.emarketer.com/content/do-most-searchers-really-start-on-amazon.

Feedvisor (2020). Amazon 1P vs. 3P: What are the differences? Feedvisor, 3 December. https://feedvisor.com/university/amazon-1p-vs-3p/.

Herrera, R. (2019). Amazon PPC challenges Google Ads. *Insignia*, 3 April. https://insigniaseo.com/blog/amazon-ppc-challenges-google-ads.

Macrotrends (2020a). Amazon market cap 2006–2020|AMZN. *Macrotrends*, 2 December. https://www.macrotrends.net/stocks/charts/AMZN/amazon/market-cap.

Macrotrends (2020b). Amazon revenue 2006–2020|AMZN. *Macrotrends*, 1 October. https://www.macrotrends.net/stocks/charts/AMZN/amazon/revenue.

Statistics TIMES (2020). List of countries by GDP. *Statistics TIMES*, 12 January. http://statisticstimes.com/economy/countries-by-gdp.php.

Thomson, J. and Hansen, J. (2016). *The Amazon Marketplace Dilemma*. Lindon, UT: Buy Box Experts.

11
Sector Impact

The realities of an interconnected global world have resulted in increased economic integration, but globalization has also brought an important conceptual change in the way we think about almost everything. Conversations in an environment of constant change, instant information, and confusing rhetoric tend to be focused on symptoms currently in front of our face or in the category of breaking news. The realities of living in a world that is increasingly connected, instantly aware, and commonly influenced by technology-driven change is much more complex. This chapter reports on thinking about the impact of change on varied sectors. The focus will be on megatrends that affect global and local constructs of business and lifestyle.

Overview

We begin with an examination of the perception of water as a resource that is not just essential for human life but also for development, health, food, and energy production. As a key resource for current and future stability, energy has seen a dramatic change as the industry is pressured by demand for environmental accountability, technological competitiveness, operational efficiency, and cultural sensitivity. The speed of change has too often made education a lagging indicator of demand. It has been plagued by ideologies, cultural mores, and parochial thinking that have led to myopic strategies even in the midst of an information explosion.

Healthcare is on top of the agenda for governments as well as being essential for people around the world. A tremendous amount of money is spent on healthcare. The presence of innovative

Global Business in the Age of Transformation. Mahesh K. Joshi and J.R. Klein, Oxford University Press.
© Mahesh K. Joshi and J.R. Klein 2021. DOI: 10.1093/oso/9780192847232.003.0011

technology is increasing accuracy and access that may address issues in countries with lower concentrations of healthcare workers, expanding technologies, and income inequities.

The manufacturing industry, once perceived as a blue-collar business, has become the centre for new technology and innovation. The implementation of technologies has enabled change that increases customization, speed, accuracy, and efficiency that were inconceivable a decade ago. Transportation remains a mainstay of a global system of trade in the face of links to pollution, global warming, and fatalities in human lives. Technology's impact on industries is probably most visible in this sector because of its prominence. With advances in artificial intelligence and other machine learning refinements it has the potential to have a monumental impact on economics, governance, culture, and individual lifestyles.

There is a growing economic concern about the scarcity of resources and the impact of climate change. Scarcity issues are complex and affected by numerous things including increases in global temperature, rising sea levels and radical weather fluctuation. Just these climate issues alone could make conventional models in agriculture, fishing industries, tourism, or basic subsistence complicated or unfeasible in parts of the world.

In the midst of resource scarcity, cultures, social institutions, and lifestyles will be tested by emerging economies, pursuing economic growth and experiencing escalating populations that for the first time have access to global markets, and have a common global demand for transportation amidst a changing environment.

Resource Demands

The model of accessing resources locally and globally through mutually beneficial relationships will become even more crucial for businesses and governments. Conflict and political tension, especially over resources, may occur as patterns change in the food, energy, and water sectors. Regulation, relating to environmental changes and ultimately through taxation and similar types of incentives/disincentives will be common. New industries (will be) created and existing ones revolutionized in response to energy scarcity, climate change, and lack of resources. The pace of these changes will be accelerated by new technologies (PWC, 2016).

Global demand for materials increased ten-fold during the twentieth century and is set to double again by 2030, compared to 2010 (Europa, 2020b). Demand for water, food, energy, land and minerals will continue to rise substantially, given the increasing purchasing power of a growing population. Supply bottlenecks could be further aggravated by climate change, making natural resources increasingly scarce and more expensive to source.

If present trends continue, human demand on the Earth's ecosystem is projected to exceed nature's capacity to regenerate by 100 per cent (meaning that we would need two Earth planets to meet human demands) by 2030 (SGS, 2019).

Humanity currently uses resources at a rate 50 per cent faster than they can be regenerated by nature (Europa, 2020a). The pressures of population growth, climate change, environmental degradation, and expanding influence of the East and South are placing increasing stress on finite, non-renewable resources such as fossil fuels and minerals.

Over the past fifty years, the world's population has doubled, GDP has grown ten-fold, and agricultural and industrial production has boomed. Since 1970, the world is in ecological deficit. At present, 1.7 Earth planets are needed to support humanity's annual demand on the ecosystem (SGS, 2019).

Water

Growing population, urbanization, increasing demand for agricultural and industrial production, economic growth, and climate change are putting water resources under ever-increasing strain. Water is at the core of sustainable development and is critical for socio-economic development, energy and food production, healthy ecosystems and for human survival itself. Water is also at the heart of adaptation to climate change, serving as the crucial link between society and the environment.

Water is also a rights issue. As the global population grows, there is an increasing need to balance all of the competing commercial demands on water resources so that communities have enough for their needs. In particular, women and girls must have access to clean, private sanitation facilities to manage menstruation and maternity in dignity and safety.

At the human level, water cannot be seen in isolation from sanitation. Together, they are vital for reducing the global burden of disease and improving the health, education, and economic productivity of populations (United Nations, 2019).

There is a paradigm shift of wastewater being considered a problem needing a solution—'treatment and disposal'—to becoming a solution to many problems, including water scarcity and energy by 'reuse, recycle and resource recovery', in the context of a circular economy. However, currently, over 80 per cent of global wastewater is discharged without treatment; high-income countries treat about 70 per cent of the municipal and industrial wastewater they generate; upper-middle-income countries treat about 38 per cent, lower-middle-income countries up to 28 per cent, while in low-income countries, only 8 per cent of the wastewater undergoes some kind of treatment (The World Bank, 2020).

Eutrophication, pollution due to over-enrichment of water by nutrients such as nitrogen and phosphorus, is increasing, becoming one of the leading causes of water quality impairment, loss of subaquatic vegetation, change in species composition, coral reef damage, low dissolved oxygen, and the formation of dead zones (oxygen-depleted waters) that can lead to ecosystem collapse.

Just as water problems are complicated, so is the process of deciding how to address them. The United Nations and myriad non-governmental organizations (NGO), international communities, and governments are wrestling with the solutions. The OECD, as one of these parties, has scrutinized the facets of the architecture and provided a reasonable framing of what the answer must look like.

First, any effective response must be sustained and stable over time. There is a serious mismatch between the ambitious 2030 vision (United Nations) for freshwater and sanitation management, and the fragmented international political and administrative structures that contribute to its implementation. Any new institutional arrangements need to have adequate expertise and capacity to support strategic political leadership and the effective promotion and articulation of priorities across multiple policy domains and scales. For cost reasons, we need to build as far as possible on existing institutions and capabilities, while recognizing that in their current configuration they are inadequate.

Second, any approach to water must also be coherent across geographical scales. Central governments will play a key role in helping to deliver the 2030 agenda, but there are limits to what they can achieve on their own. Cities and regions play a crucial part in securing access and managing water risks on the ground and must be key players in policy development and implementation. Trans-boundary water treaties and related country obligations add yet another dimension. In each continent, treaties and macroregional organizations are trying to federate countries and inspire convergent policies. It is a little-known fact that some 295 water treaties have been signed since 1948. Any effective architecture must reflect these 'nested' levels of governance and avoid the temptation to impose top-down solutions.

Alignment with responses to other global challenges, such as adaptation to climate change and ensuring food and energy security, will also be a crucial feature of the solution. Water is a pivotal element of the Sendai framework for disaster risk reduction. We know that sustainable water management depends on initiatives taken outside the jurisdictions in charge of water: (1) municipalities and property developers build cities, which will need secure access to water and sanitation as well as protection from water risks; (2) farmers and ministries of agriculture embark on policies and investment programmes that can affect water availability and quality for communities downstream; (3) climate policies affect the energy mix, and contribute to additional demands on water. A sustainable water future requires that decisions made in these and related fields are water-wise.

Action on water must engage the full range of stakeholders, ensuring shared responsibility across public, private, and non-profit sectors. We need to move away from mere consultation, and towards co-production of knowledge and participatory decision-making, taking into account a broader set of interests. This includes the interests of local and regional authorities, business, donor agencies, NGOs, future generations, but also newcomers or emerging players such as corporates, property developers, and long-term institutional investors. The future global water architecture needs a platform where the different levels of government and the wide range of stakeholders can share knowledge, expertise, and perspectives, and can help catalyse effective and coordinated action. This is a requisite for its legitimacy, particularly in the context of high uncertainty about future water availability and demand.

Finally, an effective response to water challenges must also be evidence-based and supported by state of the art science-policy assessments of both the challenges but also our potential response options, building on existing processes and mechanisms wherever possible (Gurría, 2017).

Energy

Affected by technologies such as machine learning, artificial intelligence, and the Internet of Things, energy is going through a massive transformation. This transformation is being driven by the needs of a growing society that must be met in a way that does not harm the environment.

As energy is transformed, its importance as a driving force towards economic and social development will grow. It is projected that, while population growth is slowing, the demand will keep growing primarily because an estimated one billion people worldwide are still without access to commercial energy. This demand cannot afford to debate the issue of which methodologies should be used. It must leave all options on the table. While fossil fuels, nuclear and hydro options dominate the mix and will for the next decades, the renewables are slowly becoming more viable. Throw in the ever-present pressure of environmental impact, existing disparities in energy supply, and growing regulatory backdrop the industry will experience a few decades of consternation.

The energy world is marked by a series of deep disparities. The gap between the promise of energy for all and the fact that almost one billion people still do not have access to electricity. The gap between the latest scientific evidence highlighting the need for ever-more rapid cuts in global greenhouse gas emissions and the data showing that energy-related emissions hit another historic high in 2018 (Chestney, 2019). The gap between expectations of fast, renewables-driven energy transitions and the reality of today's energy systems in which reliance on fossil fuels remains stubbornly high. And the gap between the calm in well-supplied oil markets and the lingering unease over geopolitical tensions and uncertainties (IEA, 2019).

These disparities represent a set of extraordinarily complex challenges. Key drivers include an increasing share of renewables and decentralized production in the energy mix following the global shift towards decarbonization as well as a rapidly growing power demand from the extensive electrification that also counts power-hungry electric vehicles, which are expected to account for 9 per cent of the world's total energy needs by 2050 (Bloomberg NEF, 2018). Each of these issues can be attacked from many different angles, but because they are so closely intertwined, tweaking individual levers to tackle them separately is not enough. With this level of complexity, thinking that one player alone holds the solution is naive at best, arrogant at worst. Multiple areas need to be addressed at the same time and, therefore, by multiple players (Mogensen, 2019). Decision-makers need to take an evidence-based view on where they stand and despite the difficulties realistically consider the implications of their choices.

Manufacturing

Labour and production costs, currency values and technology in the global manufacturing industry have been the driver of significant changes. There was a time where virtually everything was individually custom made. Hand-made, one-of-a-kind products are slow to build and expensive to buy. The era of manufacturing, however, gave people and companies the power to churn out an unprecedented number of shoes, clothing, guns, and furniture, and almost anything else, for that matter, at speeds never before possible. The history of manufacturing involves radical innovations like factories, assembly lines, sewing machines, cotton gins, steam-powered diggers, trains, coal, iron, and steel (Lisa, 2009).

There are primarily two types of manufacturing globally, high-cost areas and low-cost areas. Countries like the United States, Western Europe, and Japan that initiated manufacturing on a worldwide stage are considered high-cost areas. As cost in high-cost countries began to escalate, global markets began to see lower-cost states like Latin America, Eastern Europe, and Asia become more prominent. Current geographic shifts in the manufacturing industry have other causal factors such as energy costs, currency values, labour costs, and productivity. Fluctuations in these dynamics induce manufacturers to focus on efficiency of cost and greater productivity and to re-evaluate their footprints or consider relocation of production facilities on a global scale. It is a recent phenomenon to see traditionally low-cost countries now being part of the highest-cost countries for global manufacturing. Meanwhile, many global manufacturing companies in high-cost regions like Western Europe are now facing a slump and are closing one by one in favour of emerging economies. The new map of global manufacturing is no longer simply divided into two (IMI, 2019).

Like all other sectors, manufacturing is in the midst of a technological transformation. Globalization's great disrupter is evidenced by the adoption, in all sectors, of technological innovations that foster efficiencies. The industry is moving towards more data-driven operations, soliciting and sharing information from operators, designers, and customers on everything from concepts to installation. Manufacturers will continue to pursue better performance on assembly lines producing higher quality products by integrating robotics, remote access, strategic engineering, personalized products, fewer errors, and high safety.

Innovations like 3D printing will make processes quicker and more cost-effective. It will enable customized manufacturing that will benefit the business and consumers. It will streamline processes and impact every aspect of the operation. It will reduce system setup and tooling costs, significantly reduce the cost per unit, particularly for small production runs which do not gain cost advantages through scalability. This is becoming increasingly important; a recent report found that 51 per cent of SME manufacturers are seeing customers request orders in smaller quantities (Hill, 2016). Just this one technological innovation will produce greater flexibility in production, reduced speed to market, compress design cycles, and reduce the time required to take a new product to market. There are clear benefits in technological change but they are not without challenges. The initial cost may be high and the issues of product customization may bring complexity and confusion to the market.

As manufacturing gets more technologically sophisticated, one type of labour will be decreased. However, the number of indirect jobs needed to support it will increase proportionately. Additional suppliers and new industries will emerge, powering the development of businesses beyond the factory. The investments in thought and capital to facilitate manufacturing's continued progress will produce benefit-cost, income, and market impact.

Education

The demographics of globalization indicate that the fastest-growing segment of the population in a significant portion of the world is youth. This fact alone begins to frame an alarming trend of inequity in educational access. It is estimated that 263 million children and young people are not in school with most of them living in under-developed and low- to moderate-income countries (UNESCO UIS, 2016). Other estimates report that 825 million young people will not have the basic literacy, numeracy, and digital skills to compete for the jobs of 2030 (International Commission on Financing Global Education Opportunity, 2016). Also troubling, is a notable decline in investment, financial and political, in education at all levels. The ramification of this lack of attention puts an entire generation at risk and will potentially be evidenced in instability which hobbles economic growth. Lack of access to education will constrain employment opportunities and present security risks at all levels from local to global.

Exacerbating the problem for education is the severe lack of trained educators. Many sources provide evidence that higher education is not producing the expected effects on productivity improvements, and then on economic growth and development. Investments in education and research are not effective if they cannot meet the training needs of the labour market (Castagnaa et al., 2010). Too often the university model, instead of being a crucible of thought catalysing civil discussion, becomes a bastion against change. Plagued by ideologies, cultural mores, and parochial thinking leading to myopic strategies many institutions have moved from being a facilitator of ideas to a purveyor of them. Wholesale adoption of every idea or ideology dilutes the value of the process and the relevance of the institution. The university model's dismissal of systemic change has given the message that new competitors and new technologies are irrelevant. Consumers, however, understand that their success depends on obtaining the abilities and skills to discover their place in a knowledge society. Higher education's danger in meeting this demand is that universities have new competition that has already adapted to the change.

The massive demand for innovation in education systems is reflected in the rapid growth of the marketplace gearing up to serve them. In 2017, the global educational technology market was valued at $22.8 billion and in 2019 it was $76.4 billion (Grand View Research, 2020). This is heavily skewed towards the biggest markets, namely China, India, and the United States, which have large domestic markets with common languages, large or growing middle classes with high demand for education, and significant government support (Tony Blair Institute for Global Change, 2020). In this world of technological innovation, the challenge of education is to bring equity back into the process by providing access previously unavailable to many parts of the globe.

Transportation

Emerging economies, pursuing economic growth, are experiencing escalating populations that for the first time have access to global markets, and have a common global demand for transportation. In almost every corner of the world demand for development, upgrade, or expansion of rail lines, roads, public transportation, airports, and vehicles is prevalent. Data tells us that investment in new transportation systems along with upgrades, extensions, and infrastructure is swelling globally. Also, new movement patterns for goods and people are driven by the transformation of the global economy. The egalitarian solution to the question of how to move people and cargo efficiently, safely, and sustainably without regard for social or economic status is the 'holy grail' in a progressively urbanized, digitized, and environmentally dysfunctional world.

Old thinking just will not work well anymore. Policy-makers, business strategists, and bureaucrats have to rethink their role in an increasingly complex transportation sector. The problems are many and strategists need to accept the proposition that a large number of the world's transport systems cannot meet the demands of fast-growing populations, safety, security, and accessibility. If transportation planners and policy-makers can successfully address these challenges, they will make a major contribution to improving the lives of people in all types of communities, large and small, central and remote, while at the same time protecting nature and making it possible to deliver the benefits of economic growth in a sustainable, inclusive way (Smith et al., 2019).

The transport phenomenon connects directly to the impact on fuel. BP's evolving transition scenario frames global demand for both passenger and freight transport services as more than doubling by 2040 (British Petroleum, 2020). This is mostly balanced by efficiency gains. It predicts that oil will dominate the transportation sector despite the growth of alternative fuels, particularly natural gas and electricity (British Petroleum, 2020). The scenario estimates that oil demand will account for around 85 per cent of total transport fuel demand in 2040, down from 94 per cent currently. Natural gas, electricity, and a mix of 'other' types of fuels, like hydrogen and electricity, are each projected to account for a little less than 5 per cent of transport fuel by 2040 (British Petroleum, 2020).

Changes in technology, demographics, and climate with all their complexities will continue to impact the character of the sector dramatically over the next thirty years. Decisions based on local and global perspectives will be the key to the solutions or add to the problems.

Health

The topic of health has enormous significance to people's well-being all over the world in affluent countries and the developing world. Technology's perceived impact on health tends to lean towards the innovation in machines, technologies, artificial intelligence, and the potential for robots to replace medical professionals. The reality is that the most profound changes in healthcare will initially be much simpler and closer to home. It has already begun with the introduction of new methods of collecting data, the proliferation of wireless technology, and the acceptance of wearable technologies.

The subject of healthcare as an essential need of all the world's population is at the top of the agenda for most governments. Annual spending in the global healthcare sector is projected to reach $10 trillion by 2022 (Stasha, 2021). The World Health Organization estimates there are 43 million global health workers and an estimated needs-based shortage of over 14 million by 2030 (World Health Organization, 2016). Forty-four per cent of member states report less than one physician per thousand population (World Health Organization, 2016). In the United States, with over $3.81 trillion in healthcare spending (Altarum, 2019), the wait time for physicians in major metropolitan areas over the last three years increased by 30 per cent (Sanborn, 2017). National health spending is projected to grow at an average annual rate of 5.4 percent for 2019–28 and to reach $6.2 trillion by 2028 (Centers for Medicare & Medicaid Services, 2020). One can imagine how that is extrapolated in places with lower concentrations of healthcare workers and technologies.

In terms of sector impact, it must be remembered that technology alone never solves problems. The developing discussion in healthcare is about delivering healthcare services remotely by using various telecommunication methodologies. Patients do not always need a healthcare professional in the room to receive services. In its simplest form, virtual healthcare, instead of having to have a physician or other clinician or healthcare worker physically present with a patient in a room, these services are delivered with audio and video communication on a computer, mobile phone, or tablet. These encounters can take many forms and are primarily based on wireless technology. Today commercial wireless signals reach 85 per cent of the world's population and wireless communication networks extend further than the electrical grid (Adepetun, 2020).

The application of these technologies differs by situations. It can be used for basic medical conditions like routine coughs and colds, rashes, or stomach upsets which can be handled remotely instead of through an individual doctor's office visit. In addition to basic medical encounters, patient education can be delivered through virtual health patient counselling, and behavioural health lends itself to this modality. In countries where these technologies are in place, a greater degree of sophistication is being observed. Applications like the management of chronic diseases such as heart disease, heart congestion, heart failure, and lung disease can all be managed without requiring a visit to the doctor's office. Whether battling through New York traffic or living in a remote area of Africa or Southeast Asia, this provides a dramatic healthcare advantage. For treatments such as surgery that require hospital care, much of the post-operative care can be conducted remotely without the patient having to revisit the doctor or the hospital. Following up for diagnostic tests and family inclusion in health discussions can occur remotely. These discussions can be facilitated without those family members physically being present with the patient or even in the same location.

Millions of people's needs could be met without these individuals being in a doctor's office yet there are other pertinent issues also. One of the looming issues for governments is their responsibility to provide healthcare options for their citizens. In areas where resources are in short supply, there may be an opportunity to leverage existing and developing technologies to take better advantage of existing healthcare assets whether local or global. From a business standpoint, there may be opportunity that is a bit more complicated. It requires careful focus on the particular business and the economics of it. On a global level practitioners report gaps for unique financing methodologies for those parts of the world that do not have the kinds of resources that are available in developed countries.

Current examples of virtual health's impact are in the area of natural disasters where technology has been used to augment the activity of onsite healthcare workers trying to provide services when electricity and other services were not available. Dr Bruce Leff from Johns Hopkins in an article in the *Journal of the American Medical Association* talks about an application for a smartphone (Federman et al., 2018). His study was developed and carried out in Malawi, allowed community health workers to report on adherence to tuberculosis treatment, receive guidance for action or treatment in the field, and effectively double the number of patients that were able to be seen. In another recent study concerning a prevalent condition in Cameroon, Africa that causes blindness (River Blindness), a video microscope attached to a cell phone delivered test results from a finger pinprick for analysis in three minutes. This enabled thousands of people who would otherwise go undiagnosed to be treated. It is estimated that there are around 1,200 healthcare applications currently available for cell phones ranging from recording electrical heart activity through electrocardiograms, to measuring blood sugar, blood pressure, and heart rates (Israel, 2017). Virtual health's impact is significantly enhanced by the ability to remotely monitor health data of all kinds.

These types of actual encounters or remote encounters do not require a lot of technology. What is required is the delivery of information to some location, where the data can be viewed, interpreted, and analysed by expertise that can appropriately respond with directives, intervention, and treatments. This gives way to a discussion concerning countries with disparities in resources or infrastructure and their capacity to provide service across borders. It may also relate to their financing methodology and capacity to develop private sector or private–public partnerships which would facilitate the ability to purchase services. At the end of the day, it always costs something.

The most complex part of this is the capture of information, the ability to look at the data, analyse it, and develop an action plan. The action plan often does not require complex facilities. It may be as simple as giving an injection, performing a simple test, providing a course of treatment, monitoring diet, or providing home care. In addition to the technology, there is now a clear understanding of the role social determinants play in healthcare outcomes and cost.

It is an accepted assumption that virtual health will continue to expand, become more universally available, and become more complex. There will be no place where healthcare does not exist because of the way lifestyle commodities have been distributed, wireless speed increased, and the prevalence of mobile technology such as phones. Most practitioners do not anticipate replacing doctor visits or doctors entirely. Dr Michael Nochomovitz, based at New York Presbyterian Hospital, calls the evolving hybrid 'bricks and clicks'. There will be an increasing number of things that get done remotely but for the moment, there will still be a need to go to the hospital or doctor for special procedures or tests. These changes will affect the economic balance for physicians and hospitals. Monitoring, diagnostic tests, and diagnosis will be further augmented by developing technology beyond the existing phone, watches, or wearables. These devices will be invented to function inside the body or swallowed like tablets with sensors that send information to physicians and such artificial intelligence technologies will alter how we view healthcare. Most experts agree that we will still need physicians and other clinicians. Their role may change with more team models of healthcare providers assembling information for interpretation and application of judgment. A 2019 study by FAIR Health covering the period 2014–2019, showed an increase of 1,393 per cent in non-hospital based, 'provider to patient' telehealth visits, based on commercial insurance claims. This still accounted for only 0.104 per cent of all medical claims (Nochomovitz and Sharma, 2020).

One of the risks of the digital age is having lots of data without enough information. Healthcare suffers from the data-rich/

information poor syndrome with the advent and distribution of electronic health records. Professionals have a lot of data which is difficult for physicians to manage and interpret. Adding remote monitoring and devices that are embedded or worn or swallowed could dramatically explode data to the point where it loses its value because of the lack of capacity to parse the information. Careful thought must be given to how information is distributed, triaged, and who sees it. There needs to be a protocol for managing the process. In the *Journal of the American Medical Association*, Dr Rahul Sharma and Dr Michael Nochomovitz, developed the concept of the medical virtualist (Nochomovitz and Sharma, 2018). The article proposes a unique specialist that might be differentiated by different disciplines. The medical virtualist will have to be taught how to function in an environment with no physical patient interaction. The focus of this practice will be on connecting in the same way that today's practice depends on context. Sometimes healthcare organizations, physician organizations, and countries see technology as a mandate that they are forced to use. They miss the point: the technology itself is not going to solve the problem. Technology needs to put it in the context of individual particular environments, demographics, and economics (Nochomovitz and Sharma, 2018).

Within this concept, there is an argument for the creation of standards and consistent training of different types of health workers in the skills that are needed when in virtual healthcare. Virtual access still requires an examination of the patient, the environment, their condition, and potentially engaging the patient and family as part of the assessment. The provider must understand the scope of care and limitation of doing it safely. The training must contain historical data, evaluation, and examination, combining input from laboratory data, history, and remote monitoring, and understanding the modalities of creating the intervention.

Healthcare technology itself is being accelerated by the use of technologies which blur the lines between lifestyle commodities and healthcare. People are becoming used to purchasing online, making reservations online, and getting access to information online. Why wouldn't the same be true for the interaction with their physician?

Nothing will be the same in healthcare with the impact of technology. Fundamentally, most countries will have to provide more healthcare with relatively fewer resources. They will have to leverage technology as the line between lifestyle commodities and traditional healthcare disappears. Healthcare workers at all levels will need varied training to optimize and use technologies in different situations. This thinking facilitates businesses and investors to contemplate new ideas in the sector with more innovative technological tools. And then we change again.

Every sector is impacted by the speed and depth of global change. The accelerating impacts of globalization and all of its megatrends are being felt around the world. In areas where lack of access causes alienation, it is usually the poorest countries and population groups that suffer most. Urbanization offers unparalleled opportunities, yet cities find poverty and wealth side by side, increasing inequity and making the urgency of the issue more blatant. International migration enables millions of people to pursue opportunities and reduce global disparities. However, this is true only if it happens in orderly, safe, well thought out conditions.

Whether these megatrends are harnessed to encourage a more equitable and sustainable world, or allowed to exacerbate disparities and divisions, will largely determine the shape of our common future (United Nations, Department of Economic and Social Affairs, 2020).

Bibliography

Adepetun, A. (2020). Household Internet access in urban areas twice as high as in rural. *The Guardian/Technology*, 2 December.

Altarum (2019). July 2019 health sector economic indicators briefs. *Altarum*, July. https://altarum.org/publications/july-2019-health-sector-economic-indicators-briefs.

Blanchard, E. J. and Olney, W. W. (2017). Globalization and human capital investment: Export composition drives educational attainment. *Journal of International Economics*, 106, 165–183.

Bloomberg NEF (2018). Global electricity demand to increase 57% by 2050. *Bloomberg NEF*, 4 September. https://about.bnef.com/blog/global-electricity-demand-increase-57-2050/.

British Petroleum (2020). *BP Global/Transport*. London: British Petroleum.

Castagnaa, A., Colantonio, E., Furia, D., and Mattoscio, N. (2010). Does education play a relevant role in globalization? *Procedia Social and Behavioral Sciences*, 2, 3742–50.

Centers for Medicare & Medicaid Services (2020). NHE fact sheet. *CMS. gov*, 3 December. https://www.cms.gov/Research-Statistics-Data-and-Systems/Statistics-Trends-and-Reports/NationalHealthExpendData/NHE-Fact-Sheet#:~:text=National%20health%20spending%20is%20projected%20to%20grow%20at,2019–28%20and%20to%20reach%20%246.2%20trillion%20by%20202.

Chestney, N. (2019). Global carbon emissions hit record high in 2018: IEA. *Reuters*, 25 March. https://www.reuters.com/article/us-iea-emissions-idUSKCN1R7005.

Europa (2020a). Aggravating resource scarcity. *European Commission*, 5 May. https://ec.europa.eu/knowledge4policy/foresight/topic/aggravating-resource-scarcity/raw-materials-non-renewable-resources_en.

Europa (2020b). Global demand for resources. *European Commission*, 3 December. https://knowledge4policy.ec.europa.eu/foresight/topic/aggravating-resource-scarcity/global-demand-resources-materials_en.

Federman, A., Soones, T., DeCherrie, L., Leff, B., and Siu, A. (2018). Association of a bundled hospital-at-home and 30-day postacute transitional care program with clinical outcomes and patient experiences. *Journal of the American Medical Association—Internal Medicine*, 178, 1033–41.

Grand View Research (2020). *Education Technology Market Size, Share & Trends Analysis Report by Sector (Preschool, K-12, Higher Education), by End User (Business, Consumer), by Type, by Region, and Segment Forecasts, 2020–2027*. San Francisco: Grand View Research.

Gurría, A. (2017). *Putting Water at the Centre of the Global Agenda*. New York: OECD.

Hill, C. (2016). Technological advancements in the manufacturing sector. *Hawsons*, 8 November. https://www.hawsons.co.uk/technological-advancements-manufacturing/.

IEA (2019). *World Energy Outlook 2019*. Paris: International Energy Agency.

IMI (2019). How the global manufacturing economics is shifting. *IMI*, 29 August. https://www.global-imi.com/blog/how-global-manufacturing-economics-shifting.

International Commission on Financing Global Education Opportunity (2016). The learning generation: Investing in education for a changing world. https://report.educationcommission.org/downloads/.

Israel, B. (2017). A cellphone-based microscope for treating river blindness. *Berkeley Research/University of California*, 9 November. https://vcresearch.berkeley.edu/news/cellphone-based-microscope-treating-river-blindness.

Lisa, A. (2009). History of manufacturing in America. *Stacker*, 11 September. https://thestacker.com/stories/3470/history-manufacturing-america.

Mogensen, H. M. (2019). The challenges of the energy business call for new partnerships. *Smart Energy International*, 17 October. https://www.smart-energy.com/industry-sectors/business-finance-regulation/the-challenges-of-the-energy-business-call-for-new-partnerships/.

Nochomovitz, M. and Sharma, R. (2018). Virtual care as a specialty: Reply. *Journal of the American Medical Association*, 319, 2560.

Nochomovitz, M. and Sharma, R. (2020). The medical virtualist comes of age with Covid-19. *American Association for Physician Leadership*, 4 May. https://www.physicianleaders.org/news/the-medical-virtualist-comes-of-age-with-covid-19.

PWC (2016). Five megatrends and their implications for global defense & security. *PWC*, November. https://www.pwc.com/gx/en/government-public-services/assets/five-megatrends-implications.pdf.

Sanborn, B. J. (2017). Physician appointment wait times spike, highlight growing doctor shortage, survey finds. *Healthcare Finance*, 22 March. https://www.healthcarefinancenews.com/news/physician-appointment-wait-times-spike-highlight-growing-doctor-shortage-survey-finds.

SGS (2019). Global megatrends: Climate change. *SGS*, 19 June. https://www.sgs.com/en/news/2019/06/sgs-megatrends-climate-change.

Smith, J., Clayton, E., and Hanson, D. (2019). Building sustainable, inclusive transportation systems: A framework for the future. *Strategy&*, 17 February. https://www.strategyand.pwc.com/gx/en/insights/2017/building-sustainable-transport-systems/building-sustainable-inclusive-transportation-systems.pdf.

Stasha, S. (2021). The state of healthcare industry: Statistics for 2021. *Policy Advice*, 3 December. https://policyadvice.net/insurance/insights/healthcare-statistics/.

The World Bank (2020). *Shifting Paradigms for Smarter Wastewater Interventions in Latin America and the Caribbean*. Washington, DC: The World Bank.

Tony Blair Institute for Global Change (2020). *Technology and Innovation in Global Education Systems*. London: Tony Blair Institute for Global Change.

UNESCO UIS (2016). 263 million children and youth are out of school. *UNESCO*. http://uis.unesco.org/en/news/263-million-children-and-youth-are-out-school.

United Nations (2019). WHO/UNICEF Joint Monitoring Programme for Water Supply—Sanitation and hygiene. *UN Water*, 19 June. https://www.unwater.org/publication_categories/whounicef-joint-monitoring-programme-for-water-supply-sanitation-hygiene-jmp/.

United Nations, Department of Economic and Social Affairs (2020). *World Social Report 2020*. New York: United Nations.

World Health Organization (2016). *Health Workforce Requirements for Universal Health Coverage and the Sustainable Development Goals*. Geneva: World Health Organization.

SECTION 4

LEADERSHIP CHALLENGE IN A TRANSFORMATIONAL WORLD

12
Taking a New Shape

Leaders capture the interest, passion, or the acquiescence of people and incentivize behaviour germane to the leader's agenda. Leadership is the most pressing issue of local and global environments in our time. It is not just leadership in business that is important but also in politics, governance, health, welfare, and many other spheres. Leadership is taking a new shape in what is called the hyperdynamic twenty-first century. In this new iteration, there are many questions. Has leadership become too multidimensional? Will it be collaborative and inclusive resulting in service to local people producing positive advances for society and the environment? Will it be more focused on building relationships or an autocratic approach? The shape suggests hierarchical leaders will need to re-examine their approach. Leaders may not be able to drive innovation by the blind delegation of responsibilities for communication and diversity but rather leaders will be obliged to break down walls and create open communication.

The social media of the twenty-first century is in full bloom and people want to be engaged and see transparency. Instead of being the head, leaders will need to take over the role of facilitator, respecting people and allowing the creation of communities. Environments are changing at a tremendous rate in the twenty-first century. There are new types of customers and employees, new business models, new sources of value creation, and new expectations from people overall.

Constantly Changing the Role of Leadership

This is the time when leaders must be open to ideas from different audiences and different parts of the world. To begin this thinking a

Global Business in the Age of Transformation. Mahesh K. Joshi and J.R. Klein, Oxford University Press.
© Mahesh K. Joshi and J.R. Klein 2021. DOI: 10.1093/oso/9780192847232.003.0012

moment of reflection on the role of the leaders is in order. Some concepts will shape the role and create impact for leaders in the twenty-first century.

Three distinct trends are the great influences on life on this planet. The first is people. The scope and the depth of human skill, capacity, and intelligence have been improving primarily because of technological innovations and developments over the last two centuries. As human beings, whether individually or collectively, we are able to address very complex problems and produce reasonable solutions. It is a myopic view that does not gain a sense of optimism and an awareness of progressive evolutionary accomplishments for the twenty-first century.

The second distinctive driver of the twenty-first century is globalization. At its base, globalization is the process of people coming together from different parts of the world and sharing aspects of economic and social life. Through that process, there is a lot of education, driven simply by exposure to varied content and most with positive outcomes derived from diversity. This change of perception is evident not just in organizations but at the societal level.

The third trend is the impact that technology is having on human life as it functions at all levels. The digitization of the world is changing everything including access to information, culture diversity, clothing, food, travel, work, and the workplace.

In addition to these trends—human intelligence, globalization, and technology—there are three other elements that seem to characterize twenty-first century societies. Any glance across the globe will reveal the increase in inequalities. In many cities around the world, high wealth (posh) areas exist adjacent to abject poverty and slums. The evidence of economic disparity is not an anomaly. Secondly, scientific solutions in the field of infectious diseases are no longer very effective. The solution has become the problem. The developments of antibiotics to attack germ-based and viral diseases have worked well but through natural selection or mutation, we face strains that are not affected by current antibiotics. This increases the danger of pandemics exacerbated by the fact that in today's world many more millions are travelling across the globe.

For example, the COVID-19 pandemic which began in China spread around the world in a matter of months.

Inequality and disparities in quality of life are joined by a third element. Conversations with education leaders tell us that institutional education is in a state of crisis. Few countries have managed to discover the best way to educate the next generation of citizens. Education is the big challenge that all leaders must face.

Leaders in the twenty-first century will have to address these influences of people, globalization, technology, inequality, global pandemics, and education. They will not only enjoy the positive effects of human intelligence, globalization, and technology but must also deal with the challenges of inequality, quality of life, and education.

The Characteristics of Leadership

These six influences—human intelligence, globalization, technology, inequity, scientific disease control, and educational relevance—will require leaders ready to tackle the tectonic shifts of the changing world in the twenty-first century. These are big changes and big challenges. They are, however, not the first big changes the world has seen. The process dictates that to mitigate the risk of mismatching capacity and intent a more focused discussion of the character of leadership is in order. We have to pay attention. A leader essentially captures the interest, the passion, or the acquiescence of people and motivates behaviour that supports the leader's agenda. The discussion about what makes a good leader or bad leader is primarily driven by ideology, theology, geography, chronology, cultural and moral frames of reference, and who writes the history.

People that have good leadership skills may not be considered good leaders because the situational environment and characteristics they exhibited were not fitted to the time. For example, George Washington, who is regarded almost as a saint in American history, had a leadership style that was mediocre at best but his place in history serendipitously gave him tremendous formal authority, which he parlayed into tremendous informal authority. With that character and the luxury of time, he is perceived as a good leader. At the other end of the leadership scale is Adolf Hitler. He displayed some pretty dramatic leadership skills that were unfortunately driven by an extreme ideology from which the world has not yet recovered. His timeline and abuse of formal and informal authority define him, almost universally, as a bad leader. Leadership at its core must be judged based on the performance it incentivizes and the product it generates.

Three primary baseline characteristics are the foundation blocks of an effective leader. The first characteristic is creativity and inclusivity. Effective leaders continually are looking at ways of getting things done. They are constantly inquisitive. They are by nature flexible and are always looking to learn things, unlearn things, and to relearn things. There is a basic flexibility in their character that allows them to move forward in any framework. They tend to think more about 'What if?' rather than 'No way', 'How to?' rather than 'Better not'. They understand that none of us is better than any other and no one individual is smarter than all others. They understand the value of thinking together and tend to build inclusive cultures. They set clear and realistic expectations and encourage independent thinking. They importantly allow people to fail and use failure as a learning tool.

These leaders maintain structures that foster trust between all levels of an organization or relationship. They establish clear parameters within a cultural envelope that has flexibility and inclusivity. They are always looking for higher performance. They strive for it and understand that respectful dialogue driven by critical thinking is a primary driver of higher performance.

The second characteristic of effective leaders is they are driven to deliver. They always want to know just a little bit more and look for something just a little bit better in their performance. They are always analysing the data and are willing to make decisions based upon the best information they have. They understand that there is no perfect strategy but simply a lot of strategies that are good enough. They are not afraid to change.

The critical third characteristic of a leader in the local or global context is that they visibly behave as a trusted citizen. They understand how trust works and they know someone is always watching them whether at work, in the car, at the meeting, at home, or in the social world. They understand that their word is their bond. They never make assumptions without information and never accept assumptions that are divergent from what is known and are not supported by data. They never take anything personally and always seek to be the agenda driver. These leaders always do their best based on the information available and are not afraid to change course in light of new information.

These three characteristics—creative and inclusive, the drive to deliver, and trusted behaviour—are the critical elements in becoming an inclusive transformational leader.

Leadership Character Drives Leadership Purpose

A leader's character drives their purpose, which translates not only to serving the interests of the organization but also the society. Research tells us that there are leaders who pursue agendas that often work against the interest of society. In the current environment, we daily observe the problems facing the world because of the poor performance of leaders, both political and corporate, pursuing irresponsible choices that have added to the human and environmental challenges that society faces. Bad choices lead to distrust, polarization, disagreement, rhetoric rather than dialogue, misinformation, and the cyclical nature of a man-made crisis. This cycle drives isolationism, protectionism, and hyper-nationalism all of which push away from desperately needed open communication and trust-building. Effective leaders understand that inclusivity begins on common ground around common purposes and is the only way to address issues that serve individual, organizational, and societal goals. These 'common purpose' choices are what incentivize employees and consumers, and feed civil society.

Too often the daily narrative deals with issues of climate, inequalities and wealth distribution, inequalities in the political environment, inequalities in health, and inequalities in socio-economics at all levels based on access. These are a direct result of the polarizing, myopic, deaf, and dumb cyclical nature of a man-made crisis. Effective twenty-first century leaders must have something other than this myopic view of the world. Inclusive capitalism is a brilliant idea that is meant to kick-start creative thought. The concept, supported by research, suggests that there is more to doing business than simply increasing shareholder value. Successful leadership does not negate capital gain but it thinks beyond it. Leadership needs to be thinking and seeing in all directions at the same time and seeing in four dimensions.

Leadership's Inclusive Responsibility

'The Times They Are a-Changin' is the title of a Bob Dylan song released in 1964. Though nearly sixty years old, its central message is as poignant as ever in today's world. In the current and evolving environment, we hear narratives of the wealthy becoming wealthier, increasing inequality in access, deteriorating standards of living, declining levels of trust, and loss of organizational power. Leaders in today's world face monumental challenges and pressures to maintain performance.

How did we get to this place? What has brought about the erosion of leadership that got us to where we are? Examination of these questions is meant to address the decay of leadership and incentivize thinking on strengthening leadership character.

As an example of this entropy in leadership is wealth inequality in the United States. Wealth equality and wealth distribution are big concerns around the world that have caused observable dramatic shifts in many developing countries. Historical analysis of wealth and income distribution in the United States exposes public policy, statutory, and regulatory manipulation as significant elements driving redistribution of wealth-building assets (Reich, 2015).

In the wake of the Great Crash of 1929 and the consequential Great Depression, financial laws and regulations were instituted to guard against the recurrence of another similar event. Today most of those safeguards have been abandoned. This has allowed the largest Wall Street banks to acquire unprecedented influence over the economy. For example, restrictions on interstate banking, on the intermingling of investment and commercial banking, and banks becoming publicly held corporations have led to the growth of a financial sector spawning junk-bond financing, unfriendly takeovers, private equity and 'activist' investing, and the notion that corporations exist solely to maximize shareholder value.

There has been a loosening of bankruptcy laws for large corporations, most notably airlines and automobile manufacturers, allowing them to revoke labour contracts and demand wage concessions on the threat of closures. These bankruptcy provisions have not been extended to homeowners, who are burdened by mortgage debt and owe more on their homes than the homes are worth, or to graduates (students) burdened with mountains of debt. The result has been that the risk of economic failure has shifted from being a shared community risk to a risk shouldered by working people and taxpayers (Reich, 2015).

Contract laws have been altered to require mandatory arbitration before private judges, selected by big corporations. Securities laws have been relaxed to allow insider trading of confidential information. Consequently, CEOs have used stock buybacks to boost share prices and then cash in their stock options.

Loopholes have been created in tax laws for hedge funds and private-equity fund partners, special favours for the oil and gas industry, lower marginal income-tax rates on the highest incomes, and reduced estate taxes on great wealth (Reich, 2015).

Intellectual property rights, patents, trademarks, and copyrights have been enlarged and extended. Among other things, this has created windfalls for pharmaceuticals, high tech, biotechnology, and many entertainment companies, which now preserve their monopolies for a longer period. It has meant high prices for average consumers, with the United States seeing the highest pharmaceutical costs of any advanced nation. In addition, antitrust laws have been relaxed for corporations with significant market power. This market power has simultaneously raised prices and reduced services available to average Americans.

This transformation has amounted to a redistribution of wealth upward, not a 'redistribution' in its normal definition. The government did not tax the middle class and poor and transfer a portion of their incomes to the rich. Public leaders (government) undertook the upward redistribution by altering the rules of the game.

Inequality, worldwide, has been on the increase from the late 1970s. Inequality trends since 2000 have escalated dramatically from those of the 1980s and 1990s (Hammar and Waldenström, 2020). Part of this change is due to a rise in capital income (investments) over labour income (wages/salaries). In the twenty-first century, the increasing importance of capital income over labour income has been dramatic. This capital income increase has been the story of a relatively small group of people, comprising only the top 1 per cent (Kurt, 2020).

The ensuing debate over the merits of a 'free market' versus an 'activist government' has diverted attention from how the market itself has come to be organized. That organization is different from the way it was structured a half-century ago. It is the reason why the current model is failing to deliver the widely shared prosperity it generated then. It has allowed ideologists to cling to the 'people value' rhetoric. The people value argument states that individuals are paid what they are 'worth' in the market, without examining the legal and political institutions that define the market. The repetition of this rhetoric is easily confused for a moral claim that people deserve what they are paid. This value claim is meaningful only if the legal and political institutions defining the market are morally justifiable.

It is this leadership 'character' shift that has brought about declining lifestyles, public unrest, frustration driven violence, and climate change. This shift has triggered a fundamental breakdown of trust. What has happened in the world of politics, the world of media, and the world of corporate institutions is that corporate leadership action has eroded trust. Leadership has lost its direction and eliminated society from its performance equation. As a result members of society no longer trust the institutions. They do not trust the agendas of the institutions and they do not trust the leaders. The big challenge in the twenty-first century is how to restore the framework of trust, which then becomes the basis for solving the problems that we are facing (World Economic Forum, 2020).

There exists a common narrative that technology can solve many problems that face today's world. In its current iteration technology can, at its best, service as a tool. It should be a means of informing a robust, enlightened conversation among leaders who can think within a grounded essence of responsibility and employ the technology to solve problems. For this to happen, a framework of effective leadership must be present that enables the problem-solving conversation.

Three things need to be in place. First, an institutional framework in which citizens, government institutions, private institutions, social organizations, and non-governmental organizations cooperate. Such collaboration will lead to the development of solutions that can be independently or jointly delivered. This is not a 'theoretical proposition' and is already happening in many different parts of the world.

Secondly, leaders must ask the right kind of questions. Leaders must unlearn old thinking and relearn flexibility in belief and understand that what has been learned in the past may not apply to resolving problems in a contemporary context. They must be willing to work with different consequences, talk to various segments of the society, understand the true nature of the problem, and decide the best direction to the solution.

Thirdly, leaders should make choices that will restore societies' trust in institutions and their leaders. Establishing an institutional framework of cooperation, responsible leaders and leadership, and restoration of trust provides the framework that will enable leadership to be effective in the twenty-first century.

Everyone is accountable. Trust is built through accountability. It has to be an all-hands-on-deck engagement. The change leader must signal that enterprise-wide transformation will be a collective effort, with accountability distributed throughout the organization (Ready, 2016).

Bibliography

Hammar, O. and Waldenström, D. (2020). Global earnings inequality, 1970–2018. *The Economic Journal*, 130, 2526–45.

Kurt, D. (2020). Are you in the world's top 1%? *Investopedia*, 3 June. https://www.investopedia.com/articles/personal-finance/050615/are-you-top-one-percent-world.asp.

Ready, D. (2016). 4 things successful change leaders do well. *Harvard Business Review*, 28 January.

Reich, R. (2015). The political roots of widening inequality. *American Prospect*, 28 April.

World Economic Forum (2020). 3 ways to fight corruption and restore trust in leadership. World Economic Forum, 1 December. https://www.weforum.org/agenda/2020/12/anti-corruption-transparency-restore-trust-in-leadership/.

13
Trust in a Splintered World

In the current environment, the wealthy are becoming wealthier; other people are experiencing declining wealth and lifestyles. There are issues of inequalities, terrorism, and climate change. There is a decline in trust in corporate and political leaders and organizational power. In this constantly changing environment, the issue of leadership becomes the primary focus. In this 'fracture of the world' leaders must be able to make trusted choices and understand the value of trust. Trust affects the way relationships work, the way organizations operate, the way that governments work, and the way the world operates. How countries, corporations, and individuals trust each other has a lot to do with how everything works. Trust makes the world go round.

It takes only a glance at newspaper headlines to see how trust has changed. Headlines like 'Ethics Panel Inquiry, Employees' New Motto: Trust No One, Now Who Do You Trust, Parties Betray Each Other', point to an erosion of trust which has become prevalent in many places around the world. Low trust is everywhere. It saturates our global society, our organizations, our relationships, our personal lives. It breeds distrust and suspicion, which become self-replicating, resulting in a costly, downward sequence.

Steven Covey in his book *The Speed of Trust* presents some interesting statistics. 'Trust in almost every societal institution (government, media, business, health care, churches, political parties, etc.) is significantly lower than a generation ago, and in many cases, sits at historic lows. In the United States, for example, a 2005 Harris poll revealed that only 22% of those surveyed tend to trust the media, only 8% trust political parties, only 27% trust the government, and only 12% trust big companies' (Covey and Merrill, 2018 [2006]: 11).

Global Business in the Age of Transformation. Mahesh K. Joshi and J.R. Klein, Oxford University Press.
© Mahesh K. Joshi and J.R. Klein 2021. DOI: 10.1093/oso/9780192847232.003.0013

On the organizational level, trust within companies has also sharply declined. Research shows only 51 per cent of employees have trust and confidence in senior management, 36 per cent of employees believe their leaders act with honesty and integrity, and 76 per cent of employees have observed illegal or unethical conduct on the job, which, if exposed, would seriously violate the public trust (Covey and Merrill, 2018 [2006]).

More troubling is how this downward spiral has affected personal relationships. Covey says:

> A recent survey conducted by British sociologist David Halpern (Halpern, 2017) reveals that only 34% of Americans believe that other people can be trusted. In Latin America, the number is only 23%, and in Africa, the figure is 18%. Halpern's research also shows four decades ago in Great Britain, 60% of the population believed other people could be trusted; today, it's down to 29% (Halpern, 2017). Low trust causes friction, whether it is caused by unethical behaviour or by ethical but incompetent behaviour (because even good intentions can never take the test of bad judgement). Low trust creates hidden agendas, politics, interpersonal conflict, interdepartmental rivalries, win-lose thinking, defensive, and protective communication – all of which reduce the speed of trust. Low trust slows everything – every decision, every communication, and every relationship. (Covey and Merrill, 2018 [2006]: xxv)

However, the 'good' news of Halpern's study is that some places/people seem to have discovered another path. For example, people in Scandinavia (Denmark, Sweden, and Norway) and in the Netherlands believe, 68 per cent and 60 per cent respectively, that others can be trusted. This shows that there are some higher-trust societies. Also, Mexico's figure, though low at 31 per cent, is up from 1983's 19 per cent, which indicates that it is possible to increase societal trust (Covey and Merrill, 2018 [2006]).

New York Times writer Thomas Friedman, in his book *The World is Flat*, frames the importance of trust in leadership like this: 'Without trust, there is no open society, because there are not enough police to patrol every opening in an open society. Without trust, there can also be no flat world, because it is trust that allows us to take down walls, remove barriers, and eliminate friction at borders. Trust is essential for a flat world…The ability to establish, grow, extend, and restore trust with all stakeholders, customers, business partners, investors, and co-workers, is the key leadership competency of the new global economy' (Friedman, 2005: 557). Trust is the primary element and arguably may be the very definition of character. It is character that forms the foundation of leadership. It is leadership that moves us to change.

Change Leadership

There is no longer a standard template of leadership. To generate optimum performance in a changing environment leaders must adapt their strategies from a static dictatorial model to a different approach entirely. This change of style is fundamental. Leaders need a purpose which connects with different stakeholders within society. Beyond purpose, the frame in which choices are made and strategies executed is more important. In the growing diversity of today's societies, the element of uniformity is giving way to an element of diversity. This has compelling implications for leaders. Leaders simply cannot have a uniform message for various segments of society. While common purpose shared across different stakeholders is essential to change, leaders must be in a position to adapt their message to the different segments of society. A global organization with consumer products and operations in countries around the world has a market that could vary dramatically based on geography. A wealthy country like the United States has social issues that take on different nature and definition when compared to social issues in a country in Africa. The leadership of an organization operating in the United States and Africa has to adapt the message to make sense and be meaningful to the local audience. In terms of leadership behaviour, the uniformity must be substituted by flexibility.

The second component of a leader's behaviour should be the willingness to listen. Many corporate leaders spend a lot of time trying to observe customers' behaviour in detail with the intention of learning how to make better choices. Gone are the days of sitting at a drawing board in a high-rise building designing the strategy for the market. Today's leaders must be part of the reality of the diversity of the market. They must be willing to unlearn what they have learned and relearn what they see in a new reality.

Thirdly, leaders must reflect on their set of values and refine them to reflect the views of contemporary markets and society. In the discussion frame of restoring trust, the facility for leaders to make responsible choices in an environment with larger numbers of stakeholders necessitates having values that are acceptable to contemporary society. Therefore behaviour requires a certain degree of value alignment. Leadership values must be constructed that are emblematic of the best possible choices for modern society.

The fourth aspect of behaviour is honesty, integrity, and transparency in the provision of information in society. In today's setting, there is widespread media use of sponsored information presented in the form of absolute truth. These agenda-driven pieces are highly motivating to the point that innocent members of society do not know whether the information has been paid for by corporations, institutions, or individuals. Without source disclosure, these pieces do not always represent truth and often support self-serving agendas. Leaders must be cautious that the information presented to society is transparent and honest.

Finally, leaders must present themselves as individuals who are accountable to society. They must step out of the framework of a protected environment and make themselves visible to society.

The Issue of Character

Leadership today has to address multiple forms of diversity. Intergenerational diversity is one of the biggest challenges. Intergenerational diversity exemplifies itself in terms of values systems. An international organization cannot be monocultural. The inclusive character of diversity is a key competitive advantage for global business. Is there a formula that can help leaders develop a sense of what it means to lead a highly diverse organization? The answer is probably no, but some elements or leader characteristics are essential.

First leaders must be students of diversity. If a leader lacks an appreciation or understanding of diversity they have a very low probability of success. If the space in which leaders cultivate their skills is limited to the comfort of their own environment then the view of any other culture or market diversity is detrimental. Leaders who have had exposure to multiple geographies that often represent unknown or uncomfortable values are better equipped to make valid choices. The prerequisite of being a successful leader of a diverse organization requires having tasted diversity.

Secondly, leadership should be based on the principle of bridging and integrating differences. Leaders need to suspend judgement, look for common values, and seek palatable solutions. This means being willing to nurture and value the differences that exist between age groups and across cultures.

The idea of building a trust framework is what any good diversity leader must think about and requires careful observation and introspection. How a leader fosters trust between diverse cultures—trust frameworks—is today's emblematic predictor of success.

Diversity leaders need to be chancellors of change. Most people build trust based upon face-to-face interaction and that might have something to do with visual cues. In this world of technological communication channels, more innovative strategies are needed. Statistics indicate that the costs of business rise when people do not trust each other. The chancellor of change has the role of clarifying and aligning priorities, aligning the best people fit, and establishing formal and informal processes of dissemination of information. Building an environment of conversation rather than prescription is enabled by talking to people rather than to problems. It operates from a character position that accepts the value of people. It allows a person to think for themselves, which means allowing them to fail and to learn from it.

Leaders also must be malcontents of mediocrity. They must be driven towards performance rather than control. The conversations must address 'bringing me back the solution' instead of 'do this'. Allocation of autonomy is an empowering tool while prescriptive control tends to stifle innovation and squash motivation. This leadership shares accountability rather than being the person behind the curtain driving high performance. When people understand that they are valued they tend to be more valuable. The malcontent of mediocrity understands that none of us is better than any other and no one individual is smarter than all others and the pursuit of high performance is important.

Leaders also need to be the curator of the creative. People have value within their frame of reference and therefore all people have the ability to present value to those who do not share their frame. The curator of the creative provides a leadership style that quietly teaches critical thinking by coaching not cajoling. The leader builds the capacity of the culture by opening the values of individuals to the benefit of the many.

Leaders must be continual connectors. They cannot see the world through rose-coloured glasses. They must see in four dimensions recognizing the value of diversity, always listening, empowering, respecting, and including to relearning again and again. They must connect and not tear apart and exhibit behaviour worthy of trust.

Trust makes the world go round. Without it we grow farther apart and with it we move towards an equitable and successful world.

Bibliography

Covey, S. and Merrill, R. (2018 [2006]). *The Speed of Trust: The One Thing That Changes Everything*. New York: Free Press.

Friedman, T. (2005). *The World is Flat*. New York: Farrar, Straus & Giroux.

Halpern, D. (2017). How can we rebuild trust in a UK divided by inequality and suspicion? *The i newsletter*, 8 March. https://inews.co.uk/opinion/comment/can-rebuild-trust-uk-divided-inequality-suspicion-51405.

14
Tool-Box for Change

Leaders are the primary element in navigating the complexities of the constantly changing technological and global world. They must possess or develop some unique tools and characteristics that facilitate the change journey. There are some interesting examples of the implementation of this new leadership style and its impact that have been around for some time.

In the small country of Bhutan, between India and China, with a population of only 700,000, visionary and inclusive leadership has been evident for decades. This small, underdeveloped country sandwiched between two developing economic giants with the two largest populations in the world faces a seemingly overwhelming challenge of environmental survival. Bhutan's scenic and naturally beautiful land is not the only natural resource advantage it has had over the last half-century. Bhutan is governed by monarchs and has been graced by extraordinary kings. In a tough world, their leadership qualities are evident in shaping the destiny of the country not just to survive, but also to thrive. Under the leadership of their kings, they have diligently developed the country while balancing economic growth, social development, clear environmental sustainability, and the preservation of their culture. The kings built into the Constitution a framework of good governance. They introduced the GNH concept, Gross National Happiness (Centre for Bhutan Studies & GNH, 2016). In the early 1970s, the king stated that GNH is more important than GNP (gross national product). Bhutan's GDP is around US$2 billion, which is below the net worth of several individuals around the globe (Curdy, 2020). It is amazing to observe what their $2 billion GDP has accomplished when driven by leadership's desire to establish the right ideologies,

Global Business in the Age of Transformation. Mahesh K. Joshi and J.R. Klein, Oxford University Press.
© Mahesh K. Joshi and J.R. Klein 2021. DOI: 10.1093/oso/9780192847232.003.0014

institutions, and processes. Education is free as is healthcare and that includes medicine (Curdy, 2020). The king enshrined democracy in the Constitution which includes a clause that empowers the people to impeach the king. All kings must retire at the age of 65 (Curdy, 2020). Seventy-two per cent of the country is under forest cover and in the Constitution it is stated that the mission of the country is to ensure that 60 per cent of the land will always remain forest (Curdy, 2020).

How do they do it? Bhutan has very limited resources but its people use them very carefully and astoundingly the whole country is committed and faithfully focused on the core mission of GNH. Leadership has accomplished this by continually driving the population to behave in a certain way. The message is clear: economic growth is important but must not come at the expense of environmental and cultural erosion. Bhutan has become the global biodiversity hotspot. It is the only country in the world that is carbon neutral (Kuensel, 2015). Even more, it is carbon negative, which means it is a carbon sink (GVI, 2020). Bhutan generates around 2.2 million tons of carbon dioxide but the forest cover sequesters it at three times that rate at 6.6 million tons (Awitty, 2016). Bhutan has used the natural features of the land with its steep mountains and fast flowing rivers to develop renewable energy for export to neighbouring countries. By the end of 2020, they will have offset 8.7 million tons of carbon dioxide (Board, 2020). They are enhancing efforts to become an even larger carbon dioxide sink by providing free electricity to farmers so that they do not burn firewood and they are instituting subsidies on electric vehicles and LED lights. The government is going paperless leading the concept of being a green and clean Bhutan. They are not only continually maintaining and developing forest cover but also have the awareness to connect various parts of Bhutan through a network of biological corridors to help animals move freely and not remain in one protected forest area. Ironically, their critical issue is flooding from 2,700 glacial lakes fed by glacial melting because of global warming (Hays, 2019). This is an issue that is beyond their control. Bhutan represents a rare effort driven by a right-minded leadership that has established an agenda and followed through on it.

There are multiple ways to characterize the kind of leadership evident in Bhutan. This is leadership with a strong vision of what the world should be like; it is responsible, action-driven, and it can deliver applicable solutions in difficult situations. It is all about alignment in the society, discipline, and it is about everybody, irrespective of age or social background, participating in the national mission. This is something that only the most authentic leaders can achieve. Leaders who walk the talk.

The Shift to Technology

Conversations about the inevitable shift to technology in business are more than simply viewing what is coming over the horizon: it is something that is already in full swing. Based on the accomplished shift towards technology integration there are two kinds of organizations. First are some big technology companies with leadership profiles that are somewhat a disruptive phenomenon. Leaders in these organizations tend to be younger, often in their twenties and thirties, action-oriented risk takers that use failure as a learning tool. In sharp contrast are traditional organizations where leadership profiles are more comfortable. In traditional organizations, leaders develop over time spending twenty to thirty years in the ranks and eventually become the CEO or senior leaders of the company. That is not the case in technology companies. In technology companies, it is common to see 18- or 20-year-old individuals in the top leadership roles based on some technology breakthrough that allowed the company to grow. The notion of leadership in a company where technology is the core of business is dramatically different as compared to what we find in some traditional organizations. Traditional companies' leader profile might be somebody around 40–45 years old depending on how progressive the board is. The leader's most fundamental role would be to understand the nature of the technological shift and how it is affecting the industry, the business model, and the delivery model of the organization.

If the nature of technological innovation and technical complexity in the industry is substantial then the leadership has to be able to comprehend the complexity and simplify the message of the technological change. The simplified message has to explain the impact on the organization and the employees. For example, in banking and insurance, seeing the growing use of technology in online sales, the big challenge leaders face is to predict what is going to be the next shift. What is the strategy of response to this technological change and who is going to be the mysterious competitor? A fair number of large technology companies have begun to move into sectors like banking and insurance. In a traditional organization, the core leadership role is about being able to foresee the changes, comprehending how the company should respond to sustain the performance that they are used to in their historical evolution. The game has changed. It is now all about harvesting the most imaginative ideas of everybody, whether competitor, customer, employee, or college student.

Change Itself

The examination of prevalent technology changes reminds us that the issues of change are not that different. Business has always experienced change of one kind or another. The role of businesses in this kind of rapidly changing technological environment is not that different than the role of strategically effective leaders has ever been. They need to be creative and inclusive. They need to be driven to deliver. They have to behave as trusted leaders.

This technology shift is different, however, because of the nature of the change. There are additional necessary challenges that change leaders today also have to address. They must understand the basic principles of inclusive leadership. They must not only understand the character of leadership but also the challenges in an ever-changing environment. The continual cycle of change in this technologically active world means that the environment is constantly modulating also.

Douglas Ready in an article for the *Harvard Business Review* (Ready, 2016) said: 'We know that two-thirds of large scale transformation efforts fail. But that's not a helpful piece of information unless we're looking for confirmation that this is hard, really hard.' Transformational change leaders must take time to know the culture and recognize embedded tensions and paradoxes. Smart, capable, solid professionals most often perform well in their roles until they are confronted with the embedded pressures and contradictions in the changing environment. It is not new that leaders have always faced the tension of change. What is different today is that leaders no longer have the luxury of time, which makes leading effectively more complicated.

According to Ready, the most common contradiction leaders face when driving transformation efforts is that between revitalization and normalization. At the core of every change initiative is the desire to breathe new life into the organization and revitalize ways of thinking, behaving, and working. But one change initiative often morphs into many, and before long employees become 'tired of change'. Therefore, there is a need for revitalization but a desire for normalization.

A second contradiction is that between globalization and simplification. Doing business today means doing business globally, but the complexities brought on by globalization are often in conflict with the need to make it simple for customers. Leaders struggle with creating organizational responses that address the need to master globalization while offering customers and employees simplification.

Thirdly, there is innovation versus regulation. Many organizations, particularly in the aftermath of the global financial crisis, are encumbered with trying to do business, let alone innovate, under increasingly crushing regulatory environments. This is taxing on a company's capacity to find creative approaches to solving customers' needs. As such the struggle is with the tension between the desire to boost innovation and the need to operate under increasing regulation.

Optimization versus rationalization is the fourth contradiction. Customers not only have more power today, in some industries, they seem to have all of the power. Organizations are struggling to provide solutions that are better, faster, cheaper, and increasingly customized. Leaders are caught in a seemingly endless struggle to reconcile the tension between optimizing benefits to customers while rationalizing their costs of doing business.

Finally, there is digitization versus humanization. Advanced technology is at the core of virtually every company's business model today. Entire value chains are being digitized. Yet, the onset of pervasive digitization is occurring at the same time that individuals are yearning for a sense of meaning in their organizations. Leaders are struggling with how to reconcile the increasing need for the digitization of their business models while trying to create climates that have an authentic sense of humanization—creating an overarching sense of purpose and collective ambition (Ready, 2016).

Successful transformational leaders embrace these tensions even though they make the challenge more complex. There are no easy answers; however, the leader's core commitment to reconciling these tensions is vital. That means committing to ongoing communication and listening so people know what is going on and how they might contribute to the transformation effort—knowing that they are invited to do so is paramount. This process starts with the leader and top team telling powerful and compelling stories of where the company has been, where it is now, and where it needs to go and why. But it does not end there. Senior leaders must be ready to open the flood gates allowing managers and employees closest to the client interface to surface these tensions and discuss them openly. While this might not resolve the tensions and paradoxes, it enables people to at least acknowledge that they exist, have their concerns heard, and discuss proactive ways forward together (Ready, 2016).

A good example of a transformation leader is Alan Mulally, who not only led the transformation effort for Boeing Commercial Airlines but also drove the turnaround of Ford Motor Company. Mulally would insist that Ford's transformation was not his achievement but rather the collective achievement of thousands of stakeholders, including employees, suppliers, dealers, unions, financial institutions, board members, and others. He believed deeply in his 'leading together' philosophy from his Boeing experience, but this became critical at Ford, due to the multitude of stakeholders and a political infighting culture that had become toxic. Mulally brought his top managers together weekly to assess problems and progress, through his implementation process called the Creating Value Roadmap. He met with resistance due to fear of admitting problems; he built trust with those who were brave enough to acknowledge they needed help. At every meeting, managers were asked: what have we learned by sharing concerns, making course corrections, and especially, fixing problems together? By combining a focus on implementation, making tough calls, and focusing on continuous learning, Mulally changed Ford from a waning company close to bankruptcy to one of the world's most successful automobile companies (Ready, 2016).

Leaders need to pay attention to everything. They must listen, gather data, accept impact, and be inclusive. The specifics of the process, though clear, raise a very basic question, 'What are you prepared to do?'

What Are You Prepared to Do?

A first step must be building an accountable culture. Everyone is accountable. This is not a soliloquy but needs to be a group performance with everyone having a role to play. The change leader's message must be that this is an organization-wide transformation, a collective effort with accountability distributed throughout the organization. The proof of the pudding is not in the message but the action that follows. It is not so much about the values espoused as it is about the message sent. Someone is always watching.

Secondly, an organization must be able and willing to invest in these new capacities, this new transformational environment. Change leaders must go beyond storytelling, motivation, and mobilization, and provide resources enabling the organization to win in a new environment. This might include capital improvement, process improvement, and building new talent capacities. Finally, it is not only about listening it is also about learning. Successful companies that are making transitional change work have leaders that come to terms with the concept of the relentless learning process.

Douglas Ready's article gives an example of flexibility and inclusive thinking in change leader Stephen Green. For three decades leading up to 2010, HSBC (bank) had successfully pursued a growth strategy and organizational capability that was founded upon acquisitions (Ready, 2016). However, with acquisition upon acquisition, the leaders within HSBC failed to develop a one-company culture, which made it difficult to integrate its offerings to an increasingly demanding customer base. As such, Stephen Green, HSBC's Chairman at the time, set the company on a course that called for a dramatic slowdown of acquisitions, at least until the current portfolio of companies was integrated and a culture of what Green referred to as Collective Management was cemented. This meant building new organizational capabilities based upon collaboration and client-first thinking, which not only meant developing new systems and processes but also building a collective mindset that would make aspiring to be a one-company culture a reality (Ready, 2016).

Leveraging these activities (accountability, providing resource capacity, continuous learning) while framing the transformation effort as a collective challenge to be embraced together, fuels positive change over the long haul since the transformation journey is a never-ending one for most companies today. In due course, these practices create a culture of agility and resiliency that will pay dividends into the future, as large-scale change becomes an organizational capability and not a recipe for management failure.

Pitfalls and Pragmatism

Research done by Oxford Senior Fellow Dr Lalit Johri and colleagues, in which they had conversations with a cohort of forty senior leaders from seventeen different countries, is worth examining. The research tried to identify what pitfalls leaders might experience when the organizations are going digital or when they are absorbing more technology. One of the fundamental traps for the leaders is how to pace the speed of change. Should the organization go for a big bang solution or should they opt for an incremental induction of technology? From the point of view of leadership it an organizational stability issue. The challenge is that if it goes too slow then they might be left behind in the competitive race. If it goes too fast it may destabilize the organization and also destabilize aspects of the culture, the consumer experience, employee behaviour, etc. The big challenge for leaders is how to agree on the speed of technological change inside the organization.

The second aspect identified was when companies are migrating towards technology from physical distribution to digital channels; in this case the challenge is how should the company ensure the stability in culture, beliefs, values, and behaviours. Often the installation of a digital business and delivery model means the faces of employees will no longer be visible to the consumers. A lot of business processing will migrate from the hands of employees to digital media. The delivery model of employees having a microscopic view of the business process is changing to a process done by machines or technology. This can create an imbalance in terms of human–machine relationships.

Another pitfall discovered by researchers is the implication of technology change on the structure, the policies, and the procedures of the organization. Does it mean that the company will have to provide a greater degree of autonomy to those who hold the levers of technology in their hands to provide the best customer service? Or can organizations continue with the concentration of decision-making power in the hands of some strategic role players?

Associated with the whole approach of technological shift and organizational change is the issue of redundancies. The adoption of new technologies may mean that companies with surplus employees will need to implement redundancies if the business is to remain viable. Regardless of explanations leaders might offer as to the need for redundancies, the challenge is to seek to balance the number of redundancies against the introduction of technology. Johri's research suggests that a big challenge for leaders is how to craft the internal messages for employees regarding the scope and scale of redundancies. How many people will stay? Who will be made redundant? And what kind of follow up programmes will be offered to redundant employees who may have been with the company for decades? It may not be easy for these employees to find alternative employment opportunities in the labour market. This is a delicate issue and the crafting of the internal message should include an opportunity for development of skill enhancement and upskilling for competitiveness of employees who are to be made redundant. For a company where heritage has been an important source of competitiveness the issue is whether technology will damage their reputational advantage. A heritage company with person-based relationships must assess and strategize relationships resting on the web. How will the change impact consumers' experience and behaviour? What happens when the faces of the company disappear behind the technology? Unfortunately, experience suggests there is often a degradation of customer service and absence of passion and sympathy for the customer. The resulting question is whether the technology can avert the obvious disconnect with the emotional make-up of customers.

The final research finding is the whole issue of expense ratios. It is commonly believed that technology can reduce the cost of most business models. However, the jury may still be out on this. Unless an organization is at a critical level of volume and is willing to make significant investments in making the technology safe, to say that technology can improve the cost advantage of the company should be examined closely. In some sectors, for example, there is a huge foundation of relationships, contracts, and negotiated settlements. Will the impact of technology in these organizations mean that the parties will behave differently? Does it mean that there will be weakening of the relationship? Does it mean that the companies will have to have new agreements, new forms of documentation, new ways to inform and exchange information, shifting away from face-to-face interactive conversations and negotiations to more technology-driven agreements? Another source of tension for the leadership is technologies' effect on which consumer segment the company is targeting. This is a problem in insurance companies where every kind of customer would have access to all delivery channels. Does this tension mean that there will be a diffusion or depletion in the service of customer demands?

As companies adopt new technologies there will be new regulatory provisions implemented and leaders must be willing to face a new regulatory environment. As technology begins taking over supervisory and operational leadership roles what happens to advisory and operational leadership as companies go digital? The answers lie before us.

Bibliography

Awitty, M. (2016). Bhutan: Committed to remaining carbon neutral. *PennState, GEOG 30—Our Perspectives*, 18 April. https://geog030. dutton.psu.edu/2016/04/18/bhutan-committed-to-remaining-carbon-neutral/.

Board, J. (2020). Bhutan's tree warrior: Spreading life in the world's most climate conscious nation. *CNA/Channel News Asia*, 21 October. https://www.channelnewsasia.com/news/asia/bhutan-climate-change-planting-trees-environment-12552692.

Centre for Bhutan Studies & GNH (2016). *2015 GNH Survey Report: A Compass Towards a Just and Harmonious Society*. Thimphu, Bhutan: Centre for Bhutan Studies & GNH. https://www.bhutanstudies.org.bt/a-compass-towards-a-just-and-harmonious-society-2015-gnh-survey-report/.

Curdy, A. (2020). History of GNH. *Ctrl Culture Relations*, 8 December. https://www.culture-relations.net/gross-national-happiness/history-of-gnh/.

GVI (2020). Why Bhutan is the only carbon-negative country in the world. *GVI*, May. https://www.gvi.co.uk/blog/bhutan-carbon-negative-country-world/.

Hays, B. (2019). Melting Himalayan glaciers increase risk for glacial lake outburst floods. *UPI (United Press International) Science News*, 31 December. https://www.upi.com/Science_News/2019/12/31/Melting-Himalayan-glaciers-increase-risk-for-glacial-lake-outburst-floods/8021577815908/.

Kuensel (2015). Bhutan reaffirms to remain carbon neutral. *Kuensel*, 1 October. https://kuenselonline.com/bhutan-reaffirms-to-remain-carbon-neutral/.

Ready, D. (2016). 4 things successful change leaders do well. *Harvard Business Review*, 28 January.

15
Being Introspective in an Expanding World

Twenty-first century leadership is at its core a holistic examination of changing environments, business models, economic ramifications, global and local impact, workplace, workforce, and strategies. This discussion surveys data, scrutinizes methodologies, presents opportunities, and suggests solutions through an examination of public–private synergy, entrepreneurship, and education. The final subject of discussion is the effect of the tectonic change on the individual leader. The bottom line, in a world that changes every minute, is not what happens but how the leader, as a person, handles what happens. Through the discussion of leadership character, transformational leaders, the tension and stress of change, and the tsunami of technology the unspoken elephant in the room is the psychological, emotional, mental, and spiritual impact on the leader as an individual. For leaders how important is it to lead a life of self-reflection and introspection?

The beginning of this thought process is to look at some anecdotal discussion of the effect of change on senior management. The VoiceAmerica.com business channel programme *Global Business with Mahesh Joshi* (VoiceAmerica, 2017) presents discussions on relevant topics focusing on interviews with local and global leaders. One of the programmes on leadership presented a discussion between authors Mr Joshi, J. R. Klein, and Dr Lalit Johri (Senior Fellow and Director of the Oxford Advanced Management and Leadership Program, Said Business School, University of Oxford). In that discussion, Mr Klein reflected on his fifty years in senior management and how it has changed:

Global Business in the Age of Transformation. Mahesh K. Joshi and J.R. Klein, Oxford University Press.
© Mahesh K. Joshi and J.R. Klein 2021. DOI: 10.1093/oso/9780192847232.003.0015

It is interesting for me to think about the kinds of changes in the business model specifically in the company I was with for the last 30 years. It was a financial service and social investment corporation that focused on inclusive capitalism to drive social impact and was categorized as a Community Development Financial Institution. Investments were vetted based on a triple bottom line process and a mission of stabilizing local economic systems. The methodology was to make physical and human asset-building investments that provided capital, social, and environmental return. I came to the firm after 20 years doing the same thing in a different geography. The nature of the business has a lot to do with interactions with customers, investors, governments, financial partners, and local communities. The operational model was fairly hierarchal and engaged in strategies, mechanisms, and processes used to implement that strategy. For the majority of my years as a senior leader, that process was done by a select group of individuals, primarily board and senior management. The process was normatively collection of data, analysis, strategic planning (setting directions), and the developing and implementation of those plans. This resulted in a five-year plan with annual reviews and one-year action plans. This procedure supported the hierarchal structure where authority was delegated, autonomy was granted, financial responsibilities siloed, and work tasks assigned.

Then the world changed. The financial industry like everything else was confronted with technology. There was a reticence to adopt new things or take 'adverse' operational risks. Thirty years ago when I moved to Ohio to take the CEO position, I had an interesting extended discussion on the decision to buy a fax machine and took grief for several years around the purchase of a mobile phone that was the size of a loaf of bread. The discussion was about if it was really needed and what would it add to the operational side of the business. Fast forward to today when a fax machine is almost an outmoded technology and we have seen a change in the whole environment that if not managed begins to diminish the value of people rather than focus on upgrading skills. Today's world is customer-centric with many of the things formerly done by people being performed by technologies.

Communication for example has changed dramatically. I came to Ohio based upon a particular kind of capital tool I uncovered in research that was sprouting in Ohio. I struck up a conversation with the Ohio folks by letter and then finally with phone calls. At one point in the conversation, they asked me if I was interested in coming to Ohio to further develop the concept being discussed. I was interested so they sent me a ticket in the mail. Yes, it sounds archaic and is almost unrecognizable by today's world.

The nature of change is change itself. Over the last decade, the nature of senior employees and middle management employees has changed dramatically. It is my opinion that we have seen a change in redundancies. Hierarchy depends on technologies and channels that are no longer relevant. The redundancy of a system that cyclically delegates, observes, and oversees precipitates the necessity to unilaterally and continually 're-task' people thereby building and hiding inefficiencies.

The new world calls for a different approach. Technology can deal with the operational metrics and makes the role of senior management superfluous. As with all employees in a digitized world, senior managers need to adapt and upgrade to new skill sets. It was my experience that the work team did not need to be tasked or overseen daily. We had hired them because of their skills and expertise so to apply hierarchical principles was the height of redundancy. What they did need was help thinking through how their skills fit into the culture and the mission. They needed, and needed to be, a coach, an advisor, and mentor to help with issues that might be challenging. As a senior manager, my ideas of autonomy, responsibility, and accountability had to change dramatically.

There was a time when anything that went wrong, the senior manager that took the responsibilities. The coach/mentor model does not absolve leaders of accountability but changes its definition. I realized that my employees found autonomy to be empowering and understood that with responsibility came accountability. There was resistance from senior and middle managers, which had been well seasoned or indoctrinated in the hierarchal placebo, to inculcate the value of a new strategy. The message had to be modelled at the top of the corporation before it could be accepted and adopted. The impact of the change was evident in obvious and subtle ways. Not only was being the purveyor of divine wisdom less effective than being a coach and guide but it also uncovered value points within the organization that added ideas and efficiencies hidden in the culture.

My lesson from the experience is that senior leaders have a dramatic-ally different role. Some leaders cannot make the shift but those that can change find it can be significantly more efficient, effective, and per-sonally satisfying. From a personal perspective, it hurts to change and usually only happens when it hurts less to change than to stay the same. Leaders of all sizes, shapes, and situations must embrace the idea of personal self-reflection and introspection. Knowing who we are enables us to understand why we are. (VoiceAmerica, 2017)

This narrative highlights the transformation of leadership at all levels and in all sectors. It also suggests that changes in the scope of relationships, whether personal or institutional, have ramifications for transformational approaches and significant potential impact on common issues globally. Several relational models that indicate the potential for this positive social change are already available.

Public–Private Synergy

Traditionally, governments have been tasked with implementing the agenda of delivering services to support the social welfare of society. This purpose is driven by finances available to the govern-ment. This works well in a small number of countries around the world with positive or surplus budgets. Ninety-five per cent of the countries around the globe do not enjoy surplus budgets. Most are constantly grappling with deficits and as a result, usually reduce programme funding supporting strategies that address societal wel-fare thereby providing negative impact for citizens of these coun-tries. It follows that, on the grounds of diminishing finances for governments, there is a case to be made for public–private partner-ships with the objective of creating value for stakeholders and shareholders. The argument goes beyond ensuring that societies do not live under the burden of social tensions. It speaks directly to the very survival of private organizations threatened by workforce validity resulting from decline in access to good education, water, housing, and healthcare. The universal erosion of these government services becomes a critical aspect of any healthy society.

In any social-economic system, the rationale for public–private partnerships can be framed in terms of equality of resources. There has to be an understanding of shared benefit between the public and the private sector. Not everything is bad about the public sector and not everything in the private sector is good. The public role of providing access to education, security, infrastructure (water, energy), and social housing is critical to societal health. The intent of the social agenda of most governments is good and attracts talented people into the public sector. However, its capital-driven lack of social services often becomes a pressure point that is little more than an attempt to deliver on promises made by politicians at election time. The arguable rationale is to form complementary intersections with the private sector to bring management expertise and a business-like culture, and build strong bridges of complementary advantage. The private sector gains a society that has a healthy workforce and healthy customers. Healthy customers consume more, earn more, pay more taxes, and offer more to public and private sector players. If done right it truly becomes a business to business partnership. With obvious synergy and common objectives, the twenty-first century is all about public and private companies working together to solve problems of the society.

As with most good ideas, it is leadership that plays the critical role. Private and public leaders must have a level of awareness of the advantages of working together. Observation of governments in many countries has evidenced different levels of maturity regarding the extent to which public and private players have partnerships. In some places like the United Kingdom there are high levels of maturity but in some emerging markets the level of defensiveness among civil servants and politicians is obvious. The prevalent thinking in these places is that they are perfectly capable of delivering all services. Public–private leadership is all about aligning the mindset of public sector policymakers and private sector senior leaders.

The first critical element of this partnership model is changing the mindset of leadership. The second aspect of leadership is understanding the complementary advantages of working together. The challenge is to develop a strategy that produces a hybrid DNA. This is a process of agreed thought, melding the public and private genealogy into an integrated mindset that makes the partnership advantages superior to the legacy's separate activities. The third element to be addressed is focused on policymakers. A conclusive regulatory environment must be created in which the private sector incurring capital and other types of risk will have the assurance that the rules of the game will not change. The environment must foster stability and understanding that both sectors can work together sharing resources and benefits alike. The private sector has to ensure that the community is always supportive. Historically, public–private partnership failures have been framed in terms of bad governance and poor leadership. All leadership failing to gather the support of society is destined to share the outcomes failed partnerships produce, as they would the benefits of successful ones.

Employment-Based Economy versus Entrepreneurial Basis

The economic shift driven by the technology tsunami is disruptive to most traditional industries. Companies like Uber, which started as a technology company, is now the biggest taxi company in the world. Airbnb is a software firm that has become the world's biggest hotel chain. Add to that the exponential shifts caused by artificial intelligence and machine learning that will become exponentially more adept at understanding the world. The law profession is being confronted with technologies like IBM's 'Watson'. Anyone can get free legal advice in seconds with 90 per cent accuracy (Ausman, 2017). In the medical profession, Watson is helping medical professionals and diagnosing cancer four times more accurately than human doctors diagnose (Lari, 2020). Technology is currently available that fits on a smartphone enabling consumers to scan the retina of their eye, take a blood sample, or breathe onto a sensor that identifies biomarkers that test for problems, disease, or other irregularities. The results are sent by Wi-Fi to medical professionals or more likely their machines (Allaert et al., 2020). The worldwide market for 3D printing products and services is anticipated to exceed US$40 billion by 2024. The industry is expected to grow at a compound annual growth rate of 26.4 per cent between 2020 and 2024 (Statista Research Department, 2020a).

The first autonomous self-driving cars are already on public roads and will soon be commonplace. This will be a tidal wave to hit the automobile industry and will also change the way our cities work. Because driverless vehicles will drop off passengers and move on, prime real estate now consumed by vast parking lots and unsightly garages could be freed up for more housing, parks, public plazas and open space. Autonomous vehicles could increase car-sharing, which would reduce traffic congestion and air pollution. Because the technology will allow these vehicles to travel closer together, they will take up less lane space. Planners say cities could use the extra space for bike lanes and wider sidewalks, making walking and biking safer and more appealing (Shaver, 2019).

This technology will transform industry in areas of worker safety by taking operators out of dangerous situations. It will save on labour costs and reduce carbon dioxide emissions. It will change the car insurance industry because human-caused accidents would presumably decrease. The healthcare benefits are initially reduced traffic accidents and fatalities. In addition to the human toll, car crashes have a substantial impact on economies, costing the US economy an estimated $871 billion per year. A recent McKinsey study (Bertoncello and Wee, 2015) found that autonomous vehicles and advanced driver assistance systems have the potential to reduce motor vehicle deaths by 90 per cent, saving thousands of lives and roughly $190 billion every year in healthcare costs. With the alleviation of traffic jams and increasing efficiency in traffic flow commuters can reduce travel times. According to the US Census Bureau, Americans spent a total of 29.6 billion hours commuting in 2014 (Herzog, 2016). With driverless vehicles, a portion of this commute time can be used for working, relaxing, reading, accessing entertainment, and having a better, more relaxed life (Ohio University, 2020).

The ramifications for business are enormous. Because of acceptance and access, any solution developed by business that does not work on a smartphone is simply of no value (Statista, 2020b). The workplace will change dramatically over the next twenty years. An Oxford Martin School study says 47 per cent of jobs as we know them today will disappear (Frey and Osborne, 2013). In agriculture the first hundred-dollar agricultural robots that can move into developing world countries and allow farmers to become managers rather than workers are close (Christiaensen et al., 2020). The next question becomes is the education system today training the next generation's workforce for jobs available now or skills that will be needed in the future?

Education for the Future

The first reflection needs to be on what education is and what it is not. The education model has not undergone any significant change in the last 100 years (Parr, 2012). Around the world, most countries are struggling to find answers as to what is the best way to offer educational opportunities. Few countries have managed to resolve this problem. Fundamentally, educational systems at both the secondary education level and the higher educational level have been designed to educate young people as employment seekers.

The education story of many present-day leaders in technology companies highlights the fact that a lot of them have left formal education uncompleted. They decided to venture on their own to develop imaginative ideas into successful businesses. The traditional model of feeding reactive, rather than proactive, talent into the twenty-first century economy that has become increasingly entrepreneurial is deeply failing in its mission. There must be a fundamental change in the way young people are educated. Society must create models that incentivize children to think. The model of standardization in education must be abandoned. The demand requires a more adaptive flexible curriculum. The model must contain enough flexibility in the institutional framework to educate young people in the pursuit of their passions.

Education is building tomorrow's leaders. Leadership must be based upon a sense of imagination and creativity and not necessarily on factoids learned during school days or in college. Those lessons are not irrelevant but the metric is not the important element. What is important is the capacity to apply it to life. The entire methodology and metrics for student assessment must evolve to assess value not memory. Education must become more inclusive introducing learners to multicultural creative thinking and risk-taking. The present system of education is geared towards helping young people to find very safe paths. The young minds of the twenty-first century must be able to take risks, assess changing situations, and quickly adapt. They must not be limited by dogmatic thinking processes or stereotyped solutions. This is a strong message for present-day educational leaders. The necessity is to change thinking about education.

It is ironic that many times movement to change must be facilitated by some common crisis or event that makes adoption of change a necessity rather than a choice. The year 2020 presented just that scenario. The COVID-19 pandemic has brought change onto the front burner with education moving to the top of the priority list. Millions of primary, secondary, and higher education models around the world are struggling with change. The old models simply do not work and unfortunately most systems were not ready for anything other than status quo. The blinding flash of the obvious is that change is no longer a choice. The pandemic crisis has brought only the choice of change or be replaced.

Self-Awareness

The expectation of twenty-first century leaders is significant and with it comes the sometimes unexpected companions of tension, pressure, and stress. A change leader must be transparent and honest in all endeavours including dealing with life itself. The Greek philosopher Socrates said: 'the unexamined life is not worth living'. A leader's ability to be introspective and self-aware is as important as any other characteristic or quality they possess. Mahatma Gandhi's leadership habit of silence and introspection led to the freedom movement in India. He always had one thing in mind: that action should be based on a strong rationale. This is the lifelong question that is sadly left unanswered because it is seldom asked. The question is 'why'.

The traditional model for leaders, when faced with complexity and uncertainty, is to strategize and plan about 'what' to do and 'how' to do it. Today's complexity and uncertainty are exponentially impactful and leaders must go beyond the 'what and how'. The demand for transparent, insightful, flexible, inclusive, culturally sensitive, and high-performance leaders often looks like a formula for an early grave. Effective leaders must know who they are and why they are. It is altruistic to pursue a life of introspection because it allows an understanding of self and an understanding of fitness to lead a mission in life. A gap between understanding the who and the mission leads to questions and feelings about authenticity. Gandhi was considered to be a very authentic person. He had a strong sense of mission but through his introspection spoke with a soft voice and galvanized millions of Indians.

Introspection and self-reflection help focus and calm the senses. They help the individual to understand the structure of the challenge and identify, through self-recognized value, valid potential solutions. They help the individual to develop a strong rationale of why some things are important. Knowing one's self and listening to what that knowledge says is called by some their inner voice, others their conscience, and still others the divine. Whatever the nomenclature it is a life path destined for success. Leaders in the twenty-first century need passion driven by a strong rationale based on self-confidence that they are doing the right thing.

In this age of transition, leaders must be cognizant of what is important to them. This conversation has tried to frame that as not just focus on a narrow objective of self-fulfilment. The primary revelation must be that we are all in this together as business leaders, leaders of social or cultural organizations, or leaders in our communities. The idea of inclusive thinking in all realms of life will contribute to civility, acceptance, equal opportunity, access, and a better world.

As Henry Ford said: 'Coming together is a beginning, keeping together is progress, working together is success.'

Bibliography

Allaert, F. A., Legrand, L., Carime, N. A., and Quantin, C. (2020). Will applications on smartphones allow a generalization of telemedicine? *BMC Medical Informatics and Decision Making*, 11 February. https://bmcmedinformdecismak.biomedcentral.com/articles/10.1186/s12911-020-1036-0.

Ausman, J. I. (2017). A view of the future from Mercedes Benz. *Surgical Neurology International*. https://surgicalneurologyint.com/surgicalint-articles/a-view-of-the-future-from-mercedes-benz/.

Bertoncello, M. and Wee, D. (2015). Ten ways autonomous driving could redefine the automotive world. *McKinsey & Company*, 1 July. https://www.mckinsey.com/industries/automotive-and-assembly/our-insights/ten-ways-autonomous-driving-could-redefine-the-automotive-world.

Christiaensen, L., Rutledge, Z., and Taylor, J. E. (2020). The future of work in agriculture. Policy Research Working Paper 9193. Washington, DC: The World Bank Group.

Frey, C. B. and Osborne, M. (2013). The future of employment: How susceptible are jobs to computerisation? Working paper, Oxford Martin School, University of Oxford.

Herzog, K. (2016). Americans spend 30 billion hours a year commuting. And it's killing them. *Grist*, 26 February. https://grist.org/living/americans-spend-30-billion-hours-a-year-commuting-and-its-killing-them/.

Lari, A. T. (2020). Modern science: Artificial intelligence can help diagnose your health conditions via selfies. *Health Writeups*, 29 August. https://healthwriteups.com/2020/08/29/modern-science-artificial-intelligence-can-help-diagnose-your-health-conditions-via-selfies/.

Ohio University (2020). 5 effects of the adoption of autonomous vehicles. *Ohio University*, 10 December. https://onlinemasters.ohio.edu/blog/5-effects-of-the-adoption-of-autonomous-vehicles/.

Parr, S. (2012). We know our education system is broken, so why can't we fix it? *Fast Company*, 30 March. https://www.fastcompany.com/1826287/we-know-our-education-system-broken-so-why-cant-we-fix-it.

Shaver, K. (2019). City planners eye self-driving vehicles to correct mistakes of the 20th-century auto. *The Washington Post*, 20 July. https://www.

washingtonpost.com/transportation/2019/07/20/city-planners-eye-self-driving-vehicles-correct-mistakes-th-century-auto/.

Statista (2020a). 3D printing industry—worldwide market size 2020–2024. Statista, 23 July. https://www.statista.com/statistics/315386/global-market-for-3d-printers/.

Statista (2020b). Smartphone ownership rate by country 2019. *Statista*, 26 November. https://www.statista.com/statistics/539395/smartphone-penetration-worldwide-by-country/.

VoiceAmerica (2017). Global business with Mahesh Joshi, Leadership in 21st Century Part 4. *VoiceAmerica.com*, 30 August. https://www.voiceamerica.com/episode/102074/leadership-in-21st-century-part-4.

Index

For the benefit of digital users, indexed terms that span two pages (e.g., 52–53) may, on occasion, appear on only one of those pages.